FRENCH
POLISHING

Finishing and restoring using traditional techniques

FRENCH
POLISHING

Finishing and restoring using traditional techniques

DEREK JONES

The Taunton Press

The Taunton Press
Inspiration for hands-on living®

The Taunton Press, Inc., 63 South Main Street
P.O. Box 5506, Newtown, CT 06470-5506
e-mail: tp@taunton.com

First published 2012 by
Guild of Master Craftsman Publications Ltd
Castle Place, 166 High Street, Lewes,
East Sussex BN7 1XU

Text © Derek Jones, 2012
Copyright in the Work © GMC Publications Ltd, 2012

Library of Congress Cataloging-in-Publication Data in progress
ISBN 978-1-62113-672-9

Publisher: **Jonathan Bailey**
Production Manager: **Jim Bulley**
Managing Editor: **Gerrie Purcell**
Senior Project Editor: **Wendy McAngus**
Editor: **Simon Smith**
Managing Art Editor: **Gilda Pacitti**
Designer: **Chloë Alexander**
Photographer: **Anthony Bailey**

Illustration on page 14 by Sara Krause, from *Fine Woodworking* magazine © 2010 by the Taunton Press, Inc.

Photograph on page 14 by Chen Kunstan.

Photograph on page 15 by Vijay Velji, from *Fine Woodworking* magazine © 2010 by the Taunton Press, Inc.

Illustration on page 46 by Simon Rodway.

Set in Adobe Caslon and Delicious

Color origination by GMC Reprographics
Printed and bound in China by Hung Hing Printing Co. Ltd.

About Your Safety

Working wood is inherently dangerous. Using hand or power tools improperly or ignoring safety practices can lead to permanent injury or even death. Don't try to perform operations you learn about here (or elsewhere) unless you're certain they are safe for you. If something about an operation doesn't feel right, don't do it. Enjoy the craft, but keep safety foremost in your mind whenever you're in the shop.

Contents

Introduction 8

Chapter 1
The story of French polish
Before shellac 12
What is shellac? 14
Pros and cons of shellac 17

Chapter 2
Workspace and materials
Workspace 20
Equipment 22
Polish and sealers 25
Fillers 30
Stains 33
Abrasives 39

Chapter 3
Preparing a surface for French polish
Selecting your wood 44
Surface preparation 47

Chapter 4
Stains and color
Applying stains   56
Color science   60
Filling the grain   65

Chapter 5
Applying shellac
The rubber   70
Brushwork   74
Flatting off between coats   78
Finishing off   80

Chapter 6
Cleaning and repolishing
Rejuvenating a piece of furniture   86

Solutions
Repairing old polish   94
Resolving common problems   104

Glossary   108
Suppliers   110
About the author   110
Index   111

Introduction

IT's often said that a good polisher can make a less than perfect piece of cabinet work look quite acceptable and that a bad one can just as easily ruin a fine example of craftsmanship. Although true, these are harsh words (no doubt meant to encourage folk to up their game in the finishing stakes), but in my experience, like good cabinet work, it takes a lot longer to perfect the technique than it does to learn how to do it in the first place.

The more interesting the wood, the better the results.

Fortunately there are plenty of "how to" books available on both disciplines to help you on your way. In each case, the authors impart their version of expertise; the approach that has worked for them but which may not necessarily be the right way. There is no right or wrong way once you've discovered the technique that works for you.

This is certainly the case when it comes to French polishing. I have had the good fortune to work with a number of experienced polishers but, beyond the fundamental basics, there is little parity in their methods. So it is with this as a

Removing oil from freshly laid polish shellac.

starting point that I have assembled what might be referred to as "the best of the best" techniques for French polishing. Strictly speaking not all of the tips are "text book." Like many old world crafts, these tips survive largely because they have been passed down through generations in the time-honored tradition of hands-on instruction.

You might be of the impression that achieving a good finish through French polishing is time-consuming and therefore not worth the effort. Let's dispel that myth for a start. You will certainly spend more time getting good results if you try to cut corners, that's for sure, but that's a lesson you've already learnt from cutting perfect joints. Remember that the process has been practiced commercially for around two centuries so I'd say it's pretty finely tuned. Each step of the way is designed to make the next easier and get you to the desired finish in the shortest time possible. In some instances a full-grain, full-gloss shellac finish can be achieved in a single day where alternative products are still drying and in need of a second (or third) coat.

The best piece of advice I can give is that you should learn from your own experience and spend time practicing with the products and the effects you can achieve on sample boards before tackling a live project. It sounds a little obvious but, unlike other finishing methods, French polishing is quite literally a hands-on experience. With so many variables ranging from ambient working temperatures, product consistency and color accuracy, the only reliable feedback available to the user is gained by developing a combination of good hand and eye coordination.

The art of French polishing is steeped in mystery and at times its secrets appear to be as closely guarded as those of the Magic Circle. Like any new trick your first attempts will look clumsy and feel awkward, but a silky-smooth professional result is well within the reach of most craftsmen. In the meantime, of course, you've got to practice a lot, experiment constantly and be prepared to get it wrong more often than not. If this sounds a little too much like hard work, not to mention frustrating, you'd be right, but the journey will be well worth it in the end. Whether you continue to use French polishing for your work or not, you will have developed a range of skills that are transferable across all mediums where a fine eye for detail is required.

All I ask is that when you're ready to throw this particular rule book out of the window, you carry on the tradition and pass the knowledge on to someone else.

Derek Jones

The story of French polish

1

Before shellac

French polishing is a traditional way of finishing wood using a preparation containing shellac, which is a secretion from an aphid-like insect. Prior to the development of shellac polish, oil and wax finishes were widely used, although they were not the only options open to furniture makers. For example, sandarac varnish (a resin from the sandarac tree) resembles shellac in its appearance and has many of the qualities we associate with shellac: it is clear and pale in color and provides a protective layer.

The solid resin is made viscous by boiling and blending with linseed oil and, although dry to the touch, it is not as hard as shellac. Over time the varnish can become contaminated with dirt and dust, clouding the appearance of the finish and the wood beneath. This material has many uses today, primarily in the conservation of artworks but not in the finishing of furniture.

Oil finishes

If you were to ask a group of complete amateurs what they would use to seal a newly made piece of work, at least half would probably come up with linseed oil (derived from the seeds of flax plants) – and who would blame them? It certainly adds color and keeps out moisture, but that's about it. Pure oils such as linseed and tung (from the nuts of the tung tree) take a long time to dry completely, if ever, and do not form a protective layer. When they are combined with varnishes, however, things get a little better. Thin them down with a solvent and they become viscous enough to apply with a rag. Used like this, repeat layers can be applied to achieve a build-up and a good protective layer. Ready-made products are available and sold as Danish oil, hard-wax oil and teak oil.

▽ *A range of oils used to keep moisture out of wood.*

△ *Waxes are used to protect and enhance.*

Wax finishes

Wax polish, in particular beeswax, is considered the most natural of finishes for treating wood. Like the main ingredient of shellac, beeswax is also the secretion of an insect, the bee. On its own it has little ability either to enhance the appearance of wood or offer much protection. However, combined with other waxes, either mineral or vegetable, a reasonably successful polish can be achieved.

While historically accurate to use on some furniture pre-dating the use of shellac-based finishes in the early 19th century, it is not possible to build up a protective glossy shine on its own the way varnishes can. The waxes that can be buffed to a shine are hard ones – carnauba, for example – but in order for them to be applied easily they must first be blended with a solvent. These are typically white spirit (mineral spirits) or turpentine. On contact with bare wood, it is the solvent that darkens the surface and, once evaporated, the wood returns to its natural color, unless, of course, the wax has a stain added to it.

Like oil finishes, a wax polish can take years to dry, and may never fully do so, and, as such, it is a host to dirt and dust. Fortunately, it is relatively easy to remove and thus a safe product to use on old pieces. Later in this book, we will look at recipes for making your own wax polish (see page 83) so that you can fine-tune the look of your French-polished surface and add a further protective layer.

What is shellac?

With the number of man-made finishes available to professionals and home users, it is amazing that there is no real synthetic alternative to shellac. Add to this the notion that the basic recipe has not changed that much in over a hundred years and you begin to get a real sense of tradition when it comes to using a shellac finish. The basic ingredient in all shellac-based products is a secretion from an aphid-like insect *Laccifer lacca*, which is about the size of an apple pip and is native to Thailand and India. The insect feeds on sap extracted from the branches of certain trees and, during its reproductive cycle, secretes an amber-colored resinous substance called lac to form a protective cocoon for its larvae. The cycle is complete when the mature insects have died and the larvae emerge from the cocoon to seek a fresh host tree. The whole process takes around six months.

The harvesting of lac can be traced as far back as AD 250. Lac dyes were in existence long before the resin was considered as a suitable product for finishing wood. There is evidence to show that the substance was a popular finish for work produced on lathes in India before the end of the 16th century.

▲ *Larvae form a hard shell, known as stick-lac.*

By the 19th century, the demand for lac dyes was in decline following the invention of synthetic aniline dyes. Rather conveniently, it seems the Western world caught on to the benefits of lac resin as a surface finish around this time, so by the 1820s shellac was well on the way to being the preferred finish of fine-furniture makers for the next 100 years. It was finally overtaken by nitrocellulose lacquers in the 1920s.

▼ *Life cycle of the* Laccifer lacca

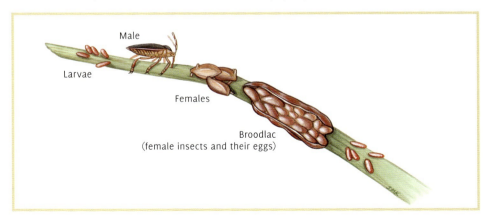

Male

Larvae

Females

Broodlac
(female insects and their eggs)

Harvesting the raw material

AFTER collecting the lac-covered branches, harvesters scrape the lac off to gather what is known as stick-lac, which contains many impurities. Further cleaning and sieving is carried out before the raw material is further refined. The final stage is to pour the resin onto a flat concrete floor and allow it to dry in the sun. The result is a product known as seed-lac because of its grain-like appearance. Colors range from lemon yellow to dark red.

The manufacturing process

SHELLAC is produced in various colors and grades, although for the most part, the means of application remains the same. The variations in color found in shellac arise from differences in the production process.

To make shellac flakes, workers pull a cooling film across the floor and hit it with a stick.

As early as the 1830s, the shellac chemists discovered a bleaching process that meant that most of the color could be removed to produce a pale-yellow varnish of great clarity. Hand-made shellac is drawn into a thin sheet to produce flakes from a molten slab about ½in (12mm) thick and 23½in (600mm) square. Machine-made shellac is a far more sophisticated affair, with the shellac made viscous either by heat or solvents and formed into sheets by rollers. If the shellac is first passed through a press filter, the wax can be extracted resulting in dewaxed shellac. Further refinement can be achieved by passing the shellac through carbon filters to extract more of the color, resulting in dewaxed and decolored shellac.

Shellac facts

Shellac is UV resistant and will not yellow or darken over time like some oil-based finishes.

Shellac will withstand exposure to water for short periods of time, so it is an ideal finish to use around the home as well as for furniture.

Shellac is less brittle than most other lacquers and therefore less likely to scratch.

Shellac adheres to practically any surface – glossy or matte.

Shellac is an all-natural product harvested regularly from the secretions of insects. It is, therefore, a renewable source.

Shellac is non-toxic and hypoallergenic.

Shellac is extremely fast drying and becomes odorless once the solvent has evaporated.

A dried film of shellac is impervious to odors and will seal in any smells.

A couple of coats of shellac will seal practically every type of unwanted stain and can be used to seal knots in soft wood prior to painting.

Shellac's natural colors mean that subtle changes in tone can be achieved as part of the process of application.

Pro Tip

How to spray shellac

It is possible to spray shellac, and some manufacturers produce products specifically for this purpose. In some cases the product will not have to be thinned, but this largely depends on the quality of your spray equipment. You can experiment by using regular shellac thinned with denatured alcohol.

This method is particularly useful when you need to finish large areas on which a traditional finish is required, such as wood-paneled walls. For a hand-finished look, you can pull the surface over with a spirit-charged rubber, or pad.

Pros and cons of shellac

Shellac polish is classed as an evaporative finish, meaning that the solvent (alcohol) has to evaporate for the finish to dry. There is no polymerization (molecular bonding), so it can be redissolved by the original solvent at any time, thus making it a reversible process. This also means that any subsequent layers applied will bond with previous layers. All this makes shellac a versatile product to have at your disposal.

Shellac has a reputation for not being a hard-wearing finish, but this may have more to do with perception than reality. Sure, it is not as waterproof as some oil-based finishes or as resistant to some chemicals as modern lacquers, but no finish exposed to extreme conditions lasts for ever.

Finishes that are classed as reactive harden by reacting with air or a chemical catalyst. These include polyurethane varnishes, acrylic lacquers and solvent-based lacquers. Once hard, the process cannot be reversed easily nor will subsequent coats of the same product bond with it. Abrading the surface will undoubtedly help, but a separate layer will still be the result.

The most common example of this can be seen on varnished surfaces where the varnish is flaking off while a seemingly good coat of varnish is present beneath. Essentially this is a delaminating of the layers.

What is shellac good for?

As a sealer, shellac can be used as a protective layer over wood prior to the application of another type of finish – for example, oil, varnish, acrylic lacquer and even paint. But it is its unique glossy finish, one that epitomizes the look that we have to associate with some of the best furniture, that is its principal application. When applied using the French-polish technique, it enhances the appearance of the wood in such a way that it becomes part of the wood rather than simply floating on top of it.

When not to use it

Shellac on its own is not waterproof and so should not be used where the surface is likely to be exposed to water. This includes exterior work, kitchen work surfaces, bathroom panels and bar tops, for example. Also, shellac is likely to perish if exposed to some of the chemicals found in cosmetics.

Shellac can be applied for a number of reasons.

Same technique, different medium

Pro Tip

Usually shellac is applied with a cloth, a technique not exclusive to shellac and the process of French polishing. Oils can also be applied this way, including thinned varnish and even water-based varnishes.

Workspace and materials

2

Workspace

Having thought long and hard about what makes the ideal workspace for shellac polishing, it dawned on me that in over 30 years I have never had the luxury of working in one. I've had spaces that were sectioned off from the rest of the workshop (a basement as I recall), so relatively dust free, and I ran a polishing shop in an attic room that was bathed in good light for the entire day – although the ceiling was so high that heating it in winter was practically impossible.

ALL woodworkers are, by nature, resourceful, and polishers are no different. Yes, we can strive for the perfect environment, but unless you have built it yourself from the ground up it probably doesn't exist. The following elements are all individually important to create a good environment, but it is not crucial to have every one. To assess your workshop, mark each of the following criteria from one (low) to ten (high). If you achieve an overall score above 20, you're pretty well set up already.

Temperature and humidity

IF you have a working environment that is suitable for constructing furniture, it will also work for polishing. You can even increase the temperature a few degrees, but not so much as to have an adverse effect on the wood.

Temperature is easier to control than humidity and should be no less than 50°F (10°C) and no higher than 85°F (29°C). Radiators are the best source of heat and should be used in favor of gas heaters, as these introduce moisture to the environment and condensation in uninsulated buildings. Particular attention should be paid to the use of wood burning stoves and other heat sources that present a naked flame. Alcohol is a flammable material so appropriate measures should be taken to eliminate the risk of accidental fire.

Light

To get the best results with French polishing, it is important that you have good-quality light – and by that I mean as much natural daylight as possible. Light from side windows is preferable to light coming only from above, with a combination of the two being the best situation of all. Avoid strong sunlight at all costs, especially through glass, as the heat in summer can cause freshly laid polish to blister.

Any kind of artificial light – fluorescent, halogen or tungsten – will affect your ability to color match accurately, so ideally this part of the job should be tackled when there is sufficient daylight available.

It is possible to install "daylight" bulbs in lighting, but these cannot be relied upon to give a truly accurate representation of the real thing. Use them to add light to areas of the workshop where shadows from natural daylight occur or perhaps to highlight defects in the surface of the wood or the finish.

Air quality

WHILE few of us are immune to the pleasantly intoxicating aroma of the polishing shop, work should always be carried out in an environment that is well ventilated. Notwithstanding the health implications, your work will also benefit.

Compared with other methods of finishing, French polishing is relatively forgiving as far as dust is concerned. Alcohol-based products dry quickly, so the wet area on the surface at any one time is relatively small.

However, every attempt should be made to keep your workspace as dust free as possible. Air cleaners can be used to circulate the atmosphere and remove the minute particles that can be harmful to your health, but good general housekeeping is usually adequate. Sweep up the night before, not five minutes before you start work. Use a vacuum cleaner whenever possible, as this will remove dust from the environment completely.

If your polishing shop doubles as a general workshop most of the time, then be aware that dust and other contaminants are likely to be found lurking on exposed beams and extraction pipes so take steps to keep them clear.

Pro Tip

Keep it clean

The shelves on which you keep your polishing materials as well as the containers themselves will harbor dust. Keep them clean, because otherwise the first thing you will want to do is blow the dust off the lid when you reach for it. Get into the habit of wiping around the rim of your polishing bottles, as these too become encrusted with dry polish, which can, if you're not careful, find its way undetected onto a rubber or brush.

▼ *An air filter will circulate the air and remove tiny particles but is no substitute for good ventilation.*

Equipment

There aren't any special tools needed for carrying out French polishing, because pretty much everything that you require can be classed as everyday workshop equipment. Apart from power sanders (see page 48), the principal tool that you'll require is a good right (or left) arm. You might like to use a pair of scissors to cut through steel wool, but you should be able to find everything else already in your workshop.

Rags and cloths

You'll get through these at an alarming rate, and you can't use just any old rags. Upholstery material is generally unsuitable, as it is often non-absorbent and too thick to make into manageable handfuls. Some items of clothing are acceptable, but be sure to remove buttons and zips first.

A pad, or "rubber," is the implement used to apply shellac when a brush is not being used. This is the application method we refer to when using the term French polish. It is made out of cloth and cotton batting by the polisher and can be used more than once. The core part is referred to as a fad when used without the cloth wrap.

Fine, lint-free cotton is the only material suitable for making a rubber to apply polish, and this will need a core of skinned wadding – cotton batting that has a definite outer layer (skin) to prevent the fibers from coming apart. A good substitute for this is cotton waste, something generally available only from specialist suppliers of polishing materials and not general DIY or hardware stores. Cotton-based dishtowels are very absorbent and good for applying liquids and mopping up, but the looped type of terry cloth is less desirable, as the loops tend to catch on corners and edges.

There will be times when you need to cut back a surface, and this will inevitably create dust, perhaps when you least want it, so a small supply of tack rags will come in handy. As the name suggests, these are pieces of fine, open-weave cloth impregnated with a sticky oil used to wipe over a dusty surface and collect the dust without spreading it around.

Brushes and applicators

As well as an assortment of good-quality paintbrushes for applying stain, you will also need a couple of polishing mops. These are round-shaped, squirrel-hair brushes used only for applying shellac. Good-quality brushes aren't cheap, but if carefully looked after they will last for years. You may wish to try sponge applicators specifically designed for the application of stain. They have a pointed edge, which is handy for getting into corners. A small selection of fine-hair pencil brushes will also be required and a soft shoe brush for buffing wax.

◀ *An assortment of clean rags is essential.*

Containers and storage

Yⁿou can't beat a good supply of jelly jars for storing polish and rubbers, as well as small plastic containers for mixing up small quantities of color. Some types of plastic milk cartons can also be customized into very useful containers. For denatured alcohol, I like to use a squeezy dispenser that I bought from a laboratory-supplies warehouse. I've also found that a coffee cup is a convenient vessel into which to decant polish. They're not as easy to knock over as plastic bottles, and the handle's pretty useful too.

As some of the liquids referred to in this book are either corrosive, toxic or flammable, you must adhere to the correct standards for storage appropriate for your location. In most cases there will be a limit on the amount of flammable liquids you are permitted to store on your premises, and when not in use these should be returned to a lockable metal cabinet.

Steel wool might seem pretty harmless, but it is, in fact, highly combustible, so it needs to be kept away from sources of ignition. This includes the electrical contacts on cordless power-tool batteries.

▲ *Good-quality brushes will last for years if looked after.*

▼ *You'll find a use for practically any size of container. Clear glass is best so that colors can be easily identified.*

Make a polish boat out of old abrasive paper

1 Make two identical folds along the long edges of the sheet, approximately ½in (10mm) wide.

2 Make two identical folds across the short edges around twice the width as those along the length.

3 Bring the corners together to create walls and fold the spare paper back on itself behind the tall end.

4 Repeat this on all four corners.

5 Now fold the tall ends back down to complete the boat.

6 You now have the perfect container for mixing up small amounts of color.

Polish and sealers

Perhaps it is some of the terminology used by French polishers that gives the art an air of mystery. Words such as fad and stiffing aren't exactly commonplace, and when you consider that there are no buttons in button polish or garnet in garnet polish, it does sound a bit like a dark art. The different types of polish have their own uses within the process, so it is important to learn what the benefits of each are. The main point of difference is color, so with this in mind I shall attempt to reveal all.

EVEN the most casual reader of woodworking journals will be familiar with the term *sanding sealer*. It might be helpful at this point to make a distinction between sealer and filler because sanding sealer is used for both purposes. This shellac-based product has a cloudy appearance from the talc-like, fine powder (often zinc stearate) that is added. This performs two functions: first, to fill the grain partially and, second, to lubricate the surface while sanding after the sealer has dried. Sanding sealer is applied with a brush, and used in this way it is an alternative to wetting the wood for final sanding, as its application to bare wood will raise the grain and facilitate a smooth surface quicker than using plain shellac. This method of grain filling is best suited to work that does not require a stain.

The amount of sanding required to obtain a smooth finish can result in rubbing through the sealer to the stained surface beneath and revealing the bare wood. If the groundwork has been wetted beforehand and a stain applied, then the application of sanding sealer will provide an excellent barrier between it and the next coat. For the beginner, shellac sanding sealer should not be used to seal in spirit colors as the alcohol solvent can re-activate the stain and create uneven patches of color density.

The other type of sealer is gilding size. This product is an adhesive for gold leaf and is used extensively by sign-writers when gilding external work. In the polishing shop it can be thinned by as much as 50 per cent with mineral spirits and used as a barrier between water and spirit stains. The mixture is brushed onto the surface and the excess wiped off with a clean rag.

When using gilding size, work on small sections and don't allow it to dry beyond sticky. It is possible to reverse the drying process by wiping it over again with mineral spirits.

◀ *Sanding sealer has a cloudy appearance in the jar but is completely transparent when applied.*

Light polishes

Transparent white is a water-clear polish that has no color-changing effect whatsoever. It is especially helpful as an early-stage sealer or for building up the layer of polish where color matching is of the utmost importance.

White polish has little darkening effect, but, if used on its own over a dark stain for an entire job, there is a tendency for a gray film to be created over the work. In the absence of transparent white, it can be used toward the end of the process if the desired tone has already been reached.

Special pale is a clear golden color and useful to add body on areas that may benefit from being highlighted, such as cornices or moldings. Used without stain on light wood it imparts an almost natural wet look without too much yellowing.

Amber varnish actually does contain amber, which is first dissolved in various types of acid. This concoction is then further treated before it is combined with alcohol to be used in much the same way as shellac polish.

▼ *On dark wood a light polish will have little effect on the overall color of the piece.*

Dark polishes

Button polish is slightly yellowish and gives a golden tone. It should be avoided in any quantity over dark woods, as it tends to have a cloudy appearance and obscures the grain.

Garnet polish will give a very golden brown cast. Although cloudy in the bottle, it is clear and transparent on application.

French polish, sometimes referred to as orange polish, is lighter than garnet and button polish with a warmer tone.

▼ *Dark polishes can sometimes be rich enough in color to negate the need for a stain altogether.*

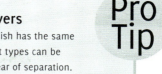

Using leftovers

As all shellac polish has the same solvent, different types can be mixed without fear of separation. This can be extremely useful when you have small amounts left over. The remnants can be used on areas that are not on show or as sealers before painting.

Guide to solvents

Product	Solvent type	Description
Ethanol	Spirit	Pure alcohol; will dissolve shellac
Methanol	Spirit	Alcohol with added poison, often referred to as denatured alcohol
Methylated spirits	Spirit	Similar to methanol but with purple dye
Mineral spirits	Oil	A product extracted from the early stage of crude oil refining and sometimes called white spirit
Naphtha	Oil	Similar to mineral spirits
Turpentine	Oil	Also similar to mineral spirits, derived from the sap of the pine tree

Solvents

BEFORE you get started, it is important to understand the difference between the two main base solvents used in the shellac polishing process: mineral spirits (petroleum based) and denatured alcohol or methylated spirits (alcohol).

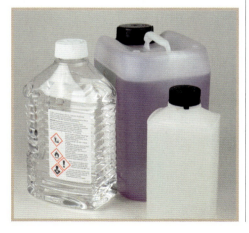

Mineral spirits is a clear, petroleum-based product that is sometimes sold as turpentine substitute. Turpentine comes from the sap of pine trees and has a very distinct smell. French polishers consider that these two products do much the same thing, although turpentine is recognized as an irritant, so is best avoided if you have not been exposed to it before.

Alcohol is the solvent for all shellac polishes. It is available as either a clear solution (denatured alcohol) or with a purple dye added (methylated spirits) to prevent it from being suitable for human consumption. Despite the purple dye, methylated spirits has no effect on the color of the polish if used to blend your own.

◀ *Left to right: mineral spirits, methylated spirit (with purple dye) and denatured alcohol.*

Adding layers

Whenever a layer of finish is applied over a previous layer of the same base solvent, there is a danger of the latter dissolving the former. If the first coat is completely dry, the risk is less but not entirely removed. For this reason it is necessary to lay on a sealing coat between layers of the same base solvent in the early stages of French polishing. See chapter 4 for more detail.

Making your own polish

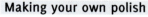

MAKING your own polish is a very simple process and, if you are not a regular user, may prove to be the most economical route. Alcohol, and therefore shellac polish, is hygroscopic (which means it takes on water molecules), so storing ready-made shellac long term is not good practice. Polish older than six months should not be used for anything other than sealing between coats of stain. To make shellac polish from scratch you need

▲ *Mix the shellac in a clear glass jar before decanting into a suitable dispensing container.*

to dissolve flakes of shellac in alcohol. This is best done overnight in an air-tight container following the instructions from the supplier and adjusting the quantities to suit your needs.

Half-and-half mixes

I used to work with a polisher who spent years French polishing in hotels and banks. A lot of the surfaces he prepared were intended for heavy use, and he therefore routinely tweaked the blend of his polish to suit the job. One recipe I picked up from him – and which he used for a bow window frame and seat – was to add amber varnish to the same quantity of sanding sealer, of which he applied two brush coats before bodying up. I've since learned that some polishers also combine amber varnish with their choice of polish to improve its resistance to the effects of moisture.

Fillers

The term *filler* refers to a variety of materials that are used in three different ways: the first is for filling the grain of the wood before sanding, the second is for repairing damaged sections of the surface prior to finishing, and the third is for making-good scratches in an existing surface finish. Although filling the grain is not essential for all wood species, it will enable you to get a smooth finish quicker, if this is the effect that you have in mind.

THE main problem with grain fillers is color matching, as most products applied to your wood will have an effect on the overall color (although clear shellac can be used this way without affecting the hue). When deciding whether or not to use filler you should take this into consideration.

There are also several materials used for disguising scratches in an existing surface finish such as wax sticks and polish revivers, often referred to as scratch removers (see page 98 for more details).

Plaster of Paris

PLASTER of Paris is a traditional product used for filling grain. The fine powder works well on fine-grained woods such as mahogany as well as coarse woods such as oak. It does require further treatment to disguise its color.

Pumice

PUMICE, a very fine volcanic glass, is also used as a pore filler. The finish grade, 4F, is used in French polishing.

Proprietary fillers

THESE are available as ready-colored blends of thick paste that are applied to the surface of the wood with a rag to fill the grain. They can also be used to minimize tonal differences in separate components of the same wood at opposing angles within a structure.

▲ *Plaster of Paris is a traditional filler.*

▶ *Proprietary fillers come in various colors.*

▲ *Mix small amounts of two-part epoxy to avoid waste.*
▼ *Wood filler is not suitable for edge work as it is easily displaced.*

▼ *Sealing wax and crayon-type waxes are very good for repairing scratches.*

Two-part epoxy

Tʜᴇsᴇ fillers are used for repairs and require you to mix two or more substances together before they can be applied. The drying time is generally quicker than single-part fillers because curing is the result of a chemical reaction. These fillers do not respond well to staining.

Wood fillers

Tʜᴇsᴇ compounds are generally water- or solvent-based clay-like substances. They do not require mixing as they rely on moisture loss into the atmosphere or substrate to harden. Unlike two-part fillers they will take a stain but can crumble easily if used on exposed edges.

Wax fillers

Wᴀx fillers can be used before you apply any finish treatment or as a repair to an existing finish. There are probably hundreds of color options available off the shelf, although they are by no means a one-stop solution, especially for large areas. They are, however, easy to apply and completely reversible if you make a mistake.

Wood glue and sawdust

Yes, the old-wives' tale is true, wood glue and sawdust do make a good filler (not PVA glue, however). This method works well on dark brown woods, but it can take on far more stain than the surrounding surface, so be careful when coloring. Hot glues gel quickly as they cool, so this little trick is best used on small areas at a time.

To be honest, unless you are considering restoration work where hide glue is likely to be the glue of choice this solution is not for you.

▶ *Sawdust from the dust bag on an electric sander can be mixed with glue to produce an impromptu filler.*

Pro Tip

Color your own filler

Although two-part fillers are available in different shades labelled generically as, for example, mahogany and light oak, in practice they often bear little resemblance to the real thing. However, you can tweak the color by adding a small amount of earth pigment to the compound before adding the hardener. You will soften the filler by adding too much, so don't overdo it, as using extra hardener won't help. Here, a light-mahogany filler has been darkened with a small amount of burnt sienna (left) to a medium mahogany (right).

Stains

The fashion for stained furniture has waned somewhat in recent years, with the preference now being for a paler, more natural look. No longer are we seduced by the thought of exotic woods from far-flung places spicing up our homes with their rich colors. In the past, stains were used to disguise cheaper cuts of wood when material costs accounted for the lion's share of the budget. Today the labor costs much the same as the materials, but the trend is for lighter-colored furniture.

STAINING may not be a skill you call on every day, but once you've learned it you can call on it when you need to. It is a technique that you can use to help show the wood off to its best advantage. And, apart from the shades that we might refer to as Jacobean or ebony, stains needn't be dark at all. In some cases, stains, in particular those used to enhance mahogany and walnut, are used to combat the inevitable loss of color caused by exposure to natural daylight.

At other times stains are used as the first step toward a pleasing natural shade of the wood itself. The job of a stain is to get as close to the finished color as possible while the wood is bare. Unlike any subsequent color-changing process, which will be partially opaque, stains tone the grain and do not hide it. The exception to this rule is ebonizing, which we will be covering in Chapter 4 (see page 63).

However, by far the most useful job carried out by staining is to homogenize the tone of multiple components in a coherent fashion. Take a stile and a rail, for example, two pieces of wood cut from the same plank to make a cabinet door. Viewed from the front, the stile, which will be placed vertically, might appear lighter than the rail that runs horizontally. Viewed from the back, and the effects might well be the exact opposite. Swap one of these components round so the back is now viewed from the front and the problem might go away. Of course, it might be worse, and this is where your skill as a polisher will help to overcome what I call the "tartan effect."

I would like to steer you away from the idea that polishes can be combined with stains to give a single-stage finish worthy of your hard work. For the most part, stains are absorbed into the wood and are generally non-reversible in that they require some serious intervention such as sanding or bleaching to eradicate the process.

The tonal color of stains can, however, be adjusted slightly after application by wiping over with a cloth impregnated with the appropriate solvent, for example mineral spirits, alcohol or water. Everything else you apply during the French-polishing process, including grain filler, will sit on the surface of the wood.

As well as understanding the color that stains will give to the finished piece, we must also consider their compatibility within the process itself, as not all mediums bond well to form a stable finish. All stains, if applied appropriately for the job in hand, are equally useful.

Color matching

Pro Tip

If an accurate color match is proving difficult to achieve just by repositioning the components in the structure, then a stain that requires mixing in the first place, such as a water-based dye, is best. Or use a diluted solution of the stain for the darker components and a neat one for the lighter sections.

◀ Oil-based stains are perhaps the most widely available.

Oil-based stains

WIDELY available to the amateur polisher for many years, oil-based stains are the type you are likely to find in your local hardware store. The oil used to suspend the pigments is of a petroleum base similar to mineral spirits. These stains can be applied with a rag, a brush or a sponge applicator but will require you to remove any excess with a clean lint-free cloth. Note that the color advertised on the can will not always be what you expect. One of the benefits of oil-based stains is that they don't raise the grain after application. They are less penetrative than water-based products but have the advantage

▼ Ready-mixed spirit stains are often more pigmented.

▲ *Spirit powders will need dissolving in alcohol before they can be used.*

of being able to be used on surfaces that have previously been finished. Wiping over the same area more than once will not significantly darken the surface. Shellac-based products can be applied directly onto this stain without any significant loss of tone.

Spirit-based stains

PRE-PREPARED spirit-based stains (also known as aniline dyes) are generally more vivid than oil-based stains and can be obtained in some really vibrant colors, modern versions being more light-fast than the old ones. The spirit in this case is alcohol, and they can be thinned with denatured alcohol. If anything, they are less forgiving than oil-based stains, as wiping over the same area will result in more color being applied – although with practice this can be made to work to your advantage. These stains dry much quicker than water- or oil-based stains, so it is difficult to maintain a wet working edge on large areas. For this reason they are not recommended for beginners. A few drops of spirit stain can be added to shellac polish to give it a tint should you anticipate the need to increase the depth of color later in the process. Spirit powders (above) can also be obtained to produce your own stain. In the pot they all look like a black powder, and when mixed they are quite intense.

Do not mix them in the immediate proximity of the work, as the fine particles can easily contaminate virgin wood by coming into contact with a less than spotless bench top and used rags. A spirit stain will require fixing before you can apply shellac with a rubber or fad.

▲ *Water-based stains will not need fixing before applying shellac.*

Water-based stains

WATER-BASED stains are reliable bases from which to begin the French-polishing process. For the best results, raise the grain with a damp cloth and sand the surface again prior to use. You can even use some spirit-based powders mixed with water to produce your own stains.

These can be made up in varying strengths to formulate a color wash. Of all the stains, water-based will take the longest time to dry, but they do not require fixing or sealing before applying shellac.

▼ *Water-based dyes can be intense and require thinning.*

Chemical staining

THE term *fuming* is given to the process of coloring wood through the use of chemicals that react with those already present in the wood itself. A small quantity of ammonia in an open jar is placed in an enclosed space along with the object to be treated. Woods with a high tannin content such as oak will take on a weathered appearance. The process is not generally associated with French polishing but it is well worth experimenting with, as the effect is virtually impossible to recreate with any other stain. This is nearest to a "dark art" of all the staining processes, as there is little to guide you other than trial and error to get the results that you want. Shellac can be applied directly to the surface without fixing or sealing.

▲ *Ammonia solution can be used to change the color of wood with a high tannin content.*

Stipples

STIPPLES are regarded by some polishers as rather coarse products for covering up repairs or blending old wood with new – and this is precisely why you should give them a chance. They are mostly produced by the user from a combination of earth pigments, gilding size and mineral spirits. They can also be used to fill the grain while adding color and sealing between spirit-based stains and shellac.

▼ *A gilding size stipple will color, seal and fill the grain.*

Pro Tip

Treatment for backs and bottoms

Traditionally the backs and bottoms of fine furniture were treated to some kind of finish or other. While they do not require protection from everyday use, their appearance can be improved with a color wash of stain or stipple. Contaminated polish or sanding sealer with denatured alcohol is a good base from which to start. Add some earth pigment to achieve a milky consistency and apply with a brush. Flatten off when dry and finish with a clear wax. If a stipple is used, this can be ragged off and left, as the gilding size will hold the pigments in place.

Abrasives

As this is a book about polishing, we will not explore in too much detail the vast number of abrasives available to woodworkers. We are mainly concerned with the surface finish that you are applying and not the surface before you start the polishing process. Strictly speaking, if shellac is applied correctly with a cloth this should negate the need for sanding back between coats, which is called de-nibbing.

UNTIL you are more experienced, you should be armed with a modest supply of fine abrasive papers (nothing lower than 240-grit) and steel wool. Abrasive paper is classified according to the size of the grit particles used. The two most common classifications are the United States CAMI (Coated Abrasive Manufacturers Institute, now part of the Unified Abrasives Manufacturers' Association) and the European FEPA (Federation of European Producers of Abrasives) "P" grade. Other systems used to grade sandpaper include the micron grade, which is generally used for very fine grits.

Aluminium oxide paper

THIS is the most widely available abrasive paper. Made up from wedge-shaped grains, it is manufactured in brown, green, pink, white and yellow and is tough and durable.

A coarse paper will leave a good key for a new finish but the scratch pattern is likely to show through.

Silicon carbide paper

SILICON carbide is a good all-round finishing paper, ideal for shellac polish, lacquer and paint finishes. The hexagonal-crystal structure helps prolong the life of the sheet, as the surface is less likely to deteriorate when folded. The dark particles can fracture and discolor light finishes, but this is more common when used on light woods prior to finishing when there is a need for a coarser abrasive.

Fine paper will clog quickly if the finish is not dry.

▲ *Steel wool is an essential aid to cutting back some shaped work.*

Steel wool

STEEL wool is useful for working irregular
shapes, including moldings and turned
sections, but it has a nasty habit of leaving little
particles behind, so be sure to remove these
from the workpiece as well as the surrounding
working area. A handful of steel wool works
like an abrasive cushion so it will not create a
flat surface. This has advantages when used on
an existing surface that may not be flat but still
requires smoothing off.

Open-weave sheets

OPEN-WEAVE abrasive sheets are particularly
effective when it comes to extracting dust
from the surface while sanding. The sheets
are best suited to surface preparation prior to
finishing, as they are generally more coarse
than regular sheet abrasives. Per sheet they are
more expensive than regular abrasives but last
much longer.

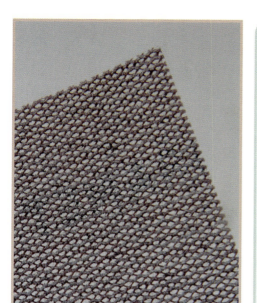

▲ *Open-weave sheet abrasive allows dust to escape.*

▼ *An average sheet of open-weave abrasive has around 1,000 perforations.*

Pro Tip

Stearated coating

Some abrasive papers are available with stearated coatings, which help to reduce the amount of waste material that clings to the paper and prolongs the life of the sheet. There is a popular theory that stearated abrasives affect the adhesion of subsequent coats when used to flatten layers of finish part-way through the process. I have never found this to be the case with alcohol, oil, water or cellulose finishes. Perhaps this stems from confusion in nomenclature. Abrasives that include "lub" or "sil" in their names seem to be a common basis for concern, as they might suggest silicone lubricants. The most likely cause of poor adhesion is failure to remove the particle build-up from the surface before applying the next coat.

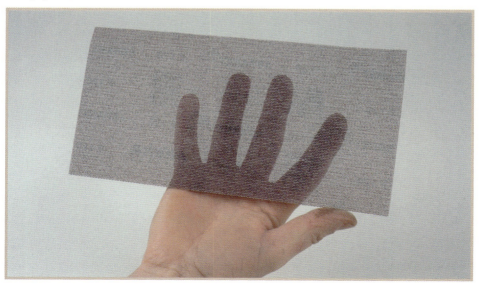

Preparing a surface
for French polish

3

Selecting your wood

One of the benefits of using shellac polishing is that you have far more control over the finished color than with any other wood finish. It is perhaps a popular misconception that shellac is for dark woods only and that, just like any other finish, it will darken the appearance of any surface to which it is applied. There are, however, techniques that can enable you to bring woods such as maple and sycamore to a full gloss shine and still retain a pure milky-white color.

Which woods are suitable for French polishing?

I CANNOT think of a wood that will not accept shellac as a finish, although some will respond better to French polishing than others. Close-grain hardwoods such as mahogany and walnut are particularly suited, as are most fruit woods. Open-grain woods – including oak, chestnut and ash – will certainly take shellac but will require a lot of grain filling if a glassy finish is to be achieved.

▼ *Most species of wood will accept shellac as a finish.*

Select the right components for an even tone and effect

I N Chapter 2 we touched on the topic of how different stains can affect the various types of grain. To minimize potential problems, it is strongly recommended that you pay some attention to wood selection.

Quarter-sawn lumber is widely accepted as the most stable cut for carcase and assembly work. On square sections such as legs or pillars, the medullary rays in oak will be present on two opposing faces. For visual continuity, position these so that they match up. This problem is less

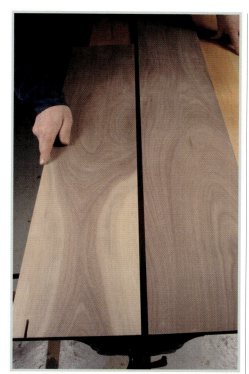

◀ *Take care when selecting boards that you can maintain visual continuity.*

this, so if this is likely to cause a problem – and to save time later – think carefully about how you can arrange the components early on in a build.

Another area where the selection of wood should be extra carefully considered is when bandings or moldings are added to the edges of veneered boards. The wood may well be of the same species, but that may be all that the two components actually have in common.

Carved panels

B Y its very nature, carved work has a fair degree of end grain visible. As this is matched with straight grain, it is unlikely that you will be able to achieve a uniform color across the piece. It is also most unlikely that you will get into all the surfaces to sand them smooth, so take this into consideration when planning your project. If you intend to use

evident in other woods until a finish is applied, but you should bear it in mind from an early stage. With experience, you will tune your eye, but a good tip is to wipe your grain over with denatured alcohol or a damp cloth, and then this will give you an idea of the tones that the different faces will take on after staining.

Ideally heart wood or sap wood should be avoided as neither will respond to staining alone to match the wood in the rest of a workpiece. For those situations where this is not possible, we will look at ways in which these can be made to blend in (see pages 56–59).

As a general rule, when stained, components that will be viewed with the grain running horizontally appear lighter than those with the grain running vertically. There is no antidote to

▶ *Coat porous woods with a 50/50 blend of sanding sealer and alcohol to lessen the absorption of stain.*

a stain and aim for a uniform color, the best method is to dilute the stain and add color later on in the process in the form of colored polish. Spirit-based stain is best in this case, so that it can be added to the polish. For really porous woods, try partially sealing them first with a half-and-half solution of sanding sealer and alcohol.

Solid panels

For the best-quality cabinet work you will no doubt have sections of the carcase made from adjoining components cut from the same plank or even from the same log.

To minimize the effects of movement in wide boards made up of multiple pieces you must position the boards in an alternating grain pattern so that movement in one board

A To minimize effects of movement, position boards in an alternating grain pattern.

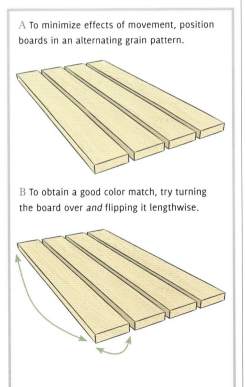

B To obtain a good color match, try turning the board over *and* flipping it lengthwise.

▲ *Invisible joints are quite possible if the grain pattern is aligned sympathetically.*

is countered by its neighbor (A, left). In doing so you might have created a light/dark pattern. To overcome this, as well as flipping the board over to the other side, rotate it along the length to reveal grain that meets the surface at the same angle as its neighbor (B, left). I can't guarantee this will work because of course we are dealing with a natural and unique material, but you can use judgment in your trial and error.

Crucial decisions such as this should always be made with the components placed together in the plane for which they are intended to be used. This means carcase sides should be assessed in the vertical and worktops in the horizontal.

Surface preparation

It is important to achieve a good flat surface for all new work because any imperfections will become really obvious as soon as a shine begins to appear. This is less important on older pieces because the surface may have distorted over time quite naturally and any attempts to correct this will be largely futile and look false. Unlike some other finishes, French polishing requires not only a smooth and flat surface but also a firm one.

THE act of applying shellac with a rubber or pad is a very physical process. Any loose moldings or delicate repairs will soon become apparent and awkward to deal with successfully after the process has begun. Think of the bare wood as having a good surface before any finishing has begun.

There is little to be gained from sanding bare wood with paper any higher than 320-grit for the majority of your polishing. Going higher can result in the burnishing of the surface, thus affecting the porosity of the wood and how well stains and sealers will bond with it. Provided the sanding is done in a controlled fashion and in sympathy with the grain pattern, 280-grit will usually be sufficient.

Small details

MOLDINGS that follow the line of an internal miter are difficult to sand right into the corner when cut and on the job.

These should therefore be finish-sanded before fitting. Likewise for any other faces that will not allow you good access after assembly – the inside faces of table legs that feature stretchers, for example, or the internal edge of a panel door.

There is, of course, an argument to be made for part-finishing these components with stain, sealer and polish before assembly but, as there is no hard-and-fast rule on this, you will have to decide what makes sense for you on any given job.

Remove hardware before polishing

Pro Tip

As far as is practical, you should remove all hardware and fittings from furniture before beginning any final sanding and finishing. Doors, drawers and knobs will all benefit from being treated individually. Resist the temptation to lubricate any moving parts before the polishing is finished. Some items of modern hardware – such as drawer runners, for example – contain grease, so be sure to remove all traces of this with mineral spirits before finishing.

Veneers

VENEERED panels have to be treated with care, as the decorative wood layer is very thin. Commercially prepared veneers are cut somewhere around 1⁄32in (0.7mm) thick so by the time you have sanded them at the cabinet-making stage you may have only a bit over 1⁄64in (0.5mm) left to play with.

Veneer is often used as a decorative feature, with burls, cross banding and quartering meeting where matching leaves from the same log are laid together as if mirrored. This presents the polisher with a problem on which direction to sand. Where the veneer has a definite grain direction this should be observed, but in the case of burls, a circular motion using the finest paper will be the best approach. The surface on burl veneer is largely made up of end grain, and during fabrication glue can seep all the way through to the finished side. This will prevent stains from taking to the surface in an even way and in extreme cases completely fill the grain, leaving you with no option but to do the same over the whole surface.

Get rid of unwanted glue

GETTING into corners to remove glue squeeze-out is tricky, so try to avoid having to do it in the first place by masking with tape any surfaces that will be hard to clean once the joint is assembled. Animal/hide glues, PVAs and aliphatic resins (carpenter's glue) are always easier to clean away when they have had time to gel slightly. The length of time it will take a glue to go off will be different for each workshop, but it is advisable to avoid rubbing glue into the grain in an attempt to clear it away. A damp cloth will help to remove PVA, and mineral spirits can be used on a rag to remove polyurethane glues.

▼ *Excess glue will become visible when stain is applied.*

Mechanical sanding

FINISHING sanders are fine to use prior to the application of shellac as long as the surface is able to withstand it. Not all sanders are suitable, though. Orbital and belt sanders can be too coarse and leave behind a visible scratch pattern.

▲ *Orbital and belt sanders can leave behind a visible scratch pattern.*

△ *Random-orbital sanders create a tight, random scratch pattern.*

△ *Linear sanders mimic the action of hand-sanding.*

Random-orbital sanders operate differently, as the abrasive pad moves off center as it rotates, creating a tight, random scratch pattern that is almost undetectable, and this type of machine is particularly useful for sanding components that come together with grain in opposing directions.

Linear sanders move in a single direction so mimic the action of hand-sanding. They can be useful for preparing thin sections, but, as with all mechanical sanders, care should be taken not to round over edges.

Ideally, when using a power sander it should be connected to a suitable dust collector.

◁ *Connect a power sander to a dust collector.*

▲ *When sanding flat areas, use a rigid block.*

Hand-sanding

EVEN with the variety of mechanical sanders to choose from there will always be a need to hand-sand some areas of your work. These will generally be moldings and edges. Flat areas will benefit from the use of a rigid block, as anything else can cause low spots invisible until the first coat of polish is applied. For sanding moldings, especially those produced on a machine, best results can be had by first producing a shaped block that matches the shape of the face of the molding.

Scraping

THERE are many purists who swear by the use of a cabinet scraper to achieve a finish fit for polish. I'm not one of them. Not because I disagree but because, unless you can treat

▶ *Moldings benefit from finish sanding before assembly.*

Pro Tip

Using card scrapers

Card scrapers can be a little tough on the thumbs as they need to be bent into a slight curve while using. For large flat areas, try using a scraper plane instead to give your thumbs a rest. Scraper planes are particularly good for flattening wood with a difficult grain.

each and every surface similarly, the rate of absorption of stain, sealer and polish will differ and so therefore will the color. Scrapers come in all shapes and sizes and can be used on flat surfaces as well as curved ones.

◀ *Cabinet scrapers can be used on molded edges.*
▼ *Flat scrapers are effective for dealing with most surfaces.*

Steaming out dents

However careful you are in the workshop, accidents do happen, but they needn't spell disaster if you know how to correct them. Dents in the surface that have not fractured the wood are generally caused by a compression of the wood fibers. This can sometimes be reversed by placing a wet dishtowel over the area and then applying a hot iron. The heat and moisture will cause the fibers to expand and return to their original shape. However, don't try this on a finished surface unless you are prepared to repair the polish as well.

If you don't have a hot iron in the workshop, try soaking a piece of cotton batting or other absorbent cloth in water and laying it on the affected area. If it keeps drying out too quickly, tape a small piece of plastic food wrap over the top to prevent the moisture from escaping.

▶ *Dents don't have to be the end of the world.*

▲ *Place a wet dishtowel over the dent and apply a hot iron.*

▲ *The heat and moisture will expand the fibers in the wood.*

▲ *Note the tramlines that have appeared on the surface caused by the compressing of wood fibers during machining.*

Wetting the surface

ANY liquid, even oils, that are applied to the surface of bare wood will raise the grain. For best results with all your polishing, French or otherwise, final preparation should always include dampening down the surface with water and allowing it to dry fully before sanding once again. This is particularly important for surfaces that have been produced on a machine, such as a planer (jointer) or molding machine.

Unlike hand tools, which are designed to slice gently through the wood, the cutters on machines are thrown at the wood with great force, which compresses the fibers, and these need to be released before any good surface can be obtained. This is especially noticeable if the cutter had a chip in its edge. Although the defect may appear to have been removed with just dry sanding, on application of the first stain it will resurface as if from nowhere. The tramlines visible in the photograph above were not obvious until dampening with water.

Pro Tip

Dust extraction

Hand-sanding will also create dust, and this can be extracted using the Abranet system from Mirka. This is particularly effective at avoiding dust contamination from dark woods to lighter ones that cannot be sanded separately, as happens with colored inlays.

Stains and color

4

Applying stains

The basis of any finishing technique where you change the color of the wood should always begin with the application of a carefully chosen stain. It is important that you get this part of the process absolutely right first time, because the chances of correcting a mistake with any real success later are extremely limited indeed. Although transparent, stains do come in varying degrees of opacity.

WATER-BASED stains in particular carry more insoluble pigments than oil- or spirit-based stains. This can be helpful if the wood has contrasting shades that need smoothing out into a single tone.

The color stated on cans of stain is not always a clear indication of how it will look when dry, as "Pine" from one manufacturer can differ quite considerably from that of another brand. It is best to test a color out and not bother too much what it says on the label. For example, an oil stain marked as "English Light Oak" can be very useful to add warmth to pale and uninteresting mahogany without further enhancing the natural red tones of the wood.

Application of any stain will cause the grain to raise.

As discussed in Chapter 3, the application of any stain (or any liquid) will cause the grain to raise, which you will naturally want to sand again so that the surface is smooth. You should hold off from any kind of surface manipulation immediately after staining until a sealing coat has been applied that is of sufficient thickness to withstand the sanding process. A sanding sealer is the preferred option in most cases.

Product compatibility

As if the choice of colors weren't enough to worry about, consideration must also be given to the base solvent of the stain. All types of stain can be used as the first stage of coloring wood for French polishing. However, unless you are an accomplished finisher, spirit-based stains require sealing with a non-alcohol-based sealer so as not to lift the stain and create patches of uneven color density. For this, a half-and-half mix of mineral spirits and gilding size is recommended, wiped on with a cloth and left to dry. For water- and oil-based stains, use shellac sanding sealer.

Blending colors

I T is possible to blend stains that have the same solvent base – although this can be a little problematic if you later need to reproduce a new mix of the color. It is quite acceptable to apply a second stain of a different solvent base provided the first coat is completely dry. This is especially useful when tinting lighter-colored wood to take on an aged appearance.

Masking off inlay

I T is unlikely that after spending many hours inlaying contrasting details or cross-banding that you will want to spoil the effect with a stain.

▶ *A spirit-based teak stain (right) was wiped over an oil-based light-oak stain (middle) to match the birch ply used in refurbishing this panel (left).*

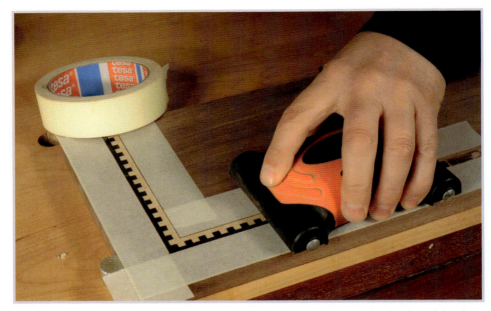

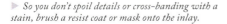 *Mask outside the inlay with tape. Press the edges down with a roller so the resist coat doesn't go beyond the inlay.*

Working up to a line is not practical, as all stains can bleed past the last stroke. The solution is to brush a resist coat or mask onto the inlay with a product that has a different solvent base from that of the stain.

Cellulose or gilding size is suitable for protecting against water- and spirit-based stains, and clear shellac can be used for oil stains. Two to three coats might be required if the inlay is particularly light or consists of end-grain material. Before doing anything, mask outside the inlay with tape and use a roller to press the edges down, because if any of your resist coat goes beyond the inlay, a nasty light patch will be evident when the stain is applied. It is worth noting that boxwood and satinwood are unaffected by exposure to ammonia, which can be used to darken both mahogany and oak, negating the need for staining altogether.

▶ *So you don't spoil details or cross-banding with a stain, brush a resist coat or mask onto the inlay.*

Where to begin with staining

A small amount of stain can travel great distances, especially into areas where it is not wanted, so always be careful when waving your brush around. Be methodical in your approach and consider the area adjacent to the one you are working on. Stain moldings first, and mop up any runs as they occur.

Treat the rails and cross members of doors before staining the styles. Work from the top down, and do not let stain collect in pockets where it will run out when the object is moved.

Color science

The science of color is a vast subject and not one that you need to become expert in to get perfectly good results when color matching wood with polish. To be blunt, we are talking about shades of brown after all (unless you are feeling particularly adventurous), and, although there are plenty to choose from, the base is always going to be a combination of red and green.

IN Solutions on page 102, we talk about colors in terms of warmth – that is, the red end of the color palette – and richness, the depth or intensity of a color, but what about the other extreme, cold and dull? These refer to the green tones and cloudiness of the finish.

Understanding colors

THE first representation of a circular color wheel was developed by Sir Isaac Newton in 1666 and remains the standard method for referencing colors today. It is based on the three primary colors – red, yellow and blue, which are colors that cannot be created by any combination of other colors (see diagram below). All other colors are derived from these.

The secondary colors (see diagram below) green, orange and purple, are produced by combining the primary colors – and this really is just about as much as you need to know to enable you to blend stains and polishes accurately. Tertiary colors are formed by mixing a primary and a secondary color.

A quick-and-easy way to get to grips with this simple color technology is first to buy a box of chocolates that come individually wrapped in Cellophane sheets. Take a piece of each of the primary colors, choosing the least intense examples available. Hold the blue and yellow up together and view into daylight, and the combination will be green. Now add the red wrapper, and the result will be brown.

If you can find more intense examples of other primary colors, experiment with these, and you will discover that red is a very powerful influence. Bear this in mind when you are mixing tints to color match because, although green will counter the effects of red, an awful lot has to be used, and the end result will be cloudy, lifeless and dull.

▼ *When primary colors (left) are combined they produce the secondary colors green, orange and purple (center). Tertiary colors (right) are formed when primary and secondary colors are combined.*

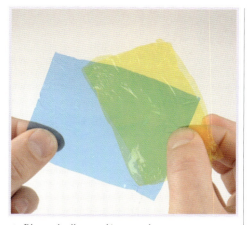

Blue and yellow combine to make green.

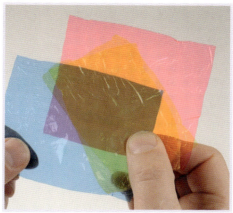

Add red and the result will be brown.

Adding color to your polish

ARMED with what you have learned from the chocolate foils, you can now begin to make a basic palette of colored shellac. I prefer to use the clearest shellac I have to hand for accuracy. Adding colors to garnet or button polish can be misleading, as there is little to identify the tint until it is on the pad and too late to change.

These polishes also have a natural color so do not allow you to read color temperature that accurately. Ready-made spirit stains can be added directly to the polish in very small quantities while spirit powders or crystals are best dissolved in alcohol before adding to the polish.

Only you can decide just how intense you need to make the colors and exactly how many variations of red and green you will require, but it is best to aim for weak solutions.

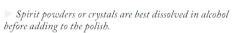

Spirit powders or crystals are best dissolved in alcohol before adding to the polish.

You can add ready-made spirit stains directly to polish.

▲ *Decide exactly how many variations of red and green you are going to need.*

▲ *Aim for weak solutions.*

Just like liquid stains, spirit powders vary in color between brands. Some powders – Vandyke brown, for example – carry extra tones, including yellow and traces of black. These are all worth experimenting with, but, once again, no two makes are exactly the same, so you will be better prepared if you also have the red and green base colors to make subtle changes in color to suit.

Adding age with a glaze

IT may be necessary to give a new piece of work the appearance of age to match original components. This can be done with a glaze onto a good ground of hard polish and is generally applied to moldings and turned work to imitate the build-up of dirt and grime. There are two ways to achieve this effect. The first requires you

to add enough spirit color to shellac to make a dark-brown polish, then add a small quantity of dark earth pigments. The mixture should be almost paint-like in opacity. Brush the glaze onto the job, working small sections at a time, and wipe over with an old rubber charged with a half-and-half solution of alcohol and shellac. This requires a deft hand, so if things get a bit sticky, stop and let the surface harden before carrying on. The rubber won't remove the glaze from the deep areas of the molding, thus creating the illusion of years of accumulated dirt.

A similar effect can be achieved by using a dark stipple made from gilding size and mineral spirits, but it will need longer to dry before applying more polish. As the working time is longer, it is perhaps easier to manage large areas this way.

▲ *Brush the stipple onto the piece you are working on, working small sections at a time.*

▲ *Wipe the excess away with a cloth leaving a moderate build-up in the corners and molding.*

If the appearance of the new polish is still too harsh, it can be muddied with a solution of Vandyke brown crystals dissolved in warm water with a small amount of soda crystals. Make sure the surface is free from any traces of oil and lightly abrade with a fine steel wool. Wipe the mixture on with a cloth, but don't allow it to puddle for too long. With a second damp cloth, wipe over the surface to leave a thin film behind. Allow the surface to dry completely before continuing with an old rubber, and spread the glaze over the surface.

Ebonizing

STAINING wood black is probably the easiest color to do – but it is just as easy to overdo and cause the surface to take on the appearance of shiny plastic. To imitate ebony, the groundwork needs to be of the finest grain structure available and porous.

The general rules apply when adding a stain, and the depth of color can be intensified by adding dye to the sanding sealer as well as the polish. It is very important not to sand completely through any layer of the process for a uniform finish to be obtained. Finish the process with a good layer of clear polish and a rubber – in bright sunshine, French, garnet and button polishes can display an orange tint if used as the base polish, so clear polish is best.

▲ *The two examples on the left (maple and beech) respond far better to black stain than those on the right (pine and ash).*

▼ *If you need to repair existing ebonized work, then two-part epoxy resin mixed with gas-black pigment makes a very good filler.*

Pro Tip

Color match in situ

Obviously, the ideal environment in which to color match is the location where the finished article will reside. In most cases this will not be possible, so, if the color is critical, it may be worth preparing a small sample on site to gauge the effects of light in situ. Generally, when working, it is nearly always most convenient to work at a comfortable bench height. However, this will not give you accurate color matching for parts of a piece that will be very high up or very low down.

Filling the grain

Woods with a coarse grain texture – such as oak or ash, for example – can have grain indents large enough to feel with your fingernail. Tight-grain woods – mahogany and walnut, for instance – have extremely fine details that feel completely smooth to the fingertips. By filling the grain you will be able to get closer to a glassy finish and achieve a more reflective surface after French polishing.

Some find this look unnatural, and when achieved with synthetic lacquers this is often the case. However, filling the grain and bringing it to a full gloss finish with shellac is something quite different and the results are unique to this process.

Finish as a filler

For fine-grain woods there is very little to be gained by the use of a grain filler. Good preparation of the surface prior to polishing with shellac will usually be sufficient to get to a full finish without much effort. However, as the shellac hardens, it will shrink back slightly, so what looks like a full finish today will need further attention tomorrow.

Proprietary fillers

Shop-bought fillers are perhaps easier to use and, with the advantage of being available in different colors, can help to minimize problems

of tone variation. They require a thorough mixing before applying to the surface with a cloth. As with plaster of Paris, the surface should be stained and sealed prior to filling.

A circular motion is best to work the compound into the grain, followed immediately with a clean cloth in straight strokes to remove the excess. Work in small areas and don't allow it to build up and dry on the surface, as you will spend a great deal of time sanding it off with the risk of leaving patchy areas behind.

Plaster of Paris

Plaster of Paris is the traditional filler, being cheap and easy to apply. The surface needs to be stained and sealed in the usual manner before using the plaster, and lightly sanded if the sealer to be used is brushed-on shellac.

To apply plaster of Paris, put some into a tub, take a damp rag and dip it into the powder. Rub the rag in a circular motion over the surface of the job, so forcing the plaster into the grain. Be sparing, and don't allow any to build up in corners. When the plaster dries it will completely obliterate the grain. Gently sanding with 240-grit or higher abrasive paper will remove the excess powder leaving the white deposits of filler only in the grain.

The filler can be made to disappear from the grain with a wipe over with boiled linseed oil. Shellac on its own will not prevent the white powder from showing up at a later date. It is important to allow the oil to dry before continuing to apply any shellac.

Pro Tip

Using grain fillers

Grain fillers are particularly helpful when dealing with large areas and places where a solid edge has been molded to expose end grain. I find that plaster of Paris works better on the more open-grained kinds of woods and on larger surfaces.

▲ Put some plaster of Paris into a tub, take a damp rag and dip it into the powder.

▼ Rub the rag in a circular motion over the surface of the job, so forcing the plaster into the grain.

Gently sand with 240-grit or higher abrasive paper to remove the excess powder.
The filler can be made to disappear from the grain with a wipe over with boiled linseed oil.

Applying shellac

5

The rubber

The key to successful French polishing is to gain complete mastery of the instrument used to apply the shellac. This is called a pad or rubber, presumably named because it is used to rub the shellac onto the surface being polished. The rubber is made out of a small section of lint-free cotton wrapped around a piece of skinned wadding. There is no right or wrong way to make it, but there are a couple of basic principles that need to be followed.

THE first important point to make is that the two materials of the rubber must be bound together so that they don't slide about; and, the second is that it should have a definite point at the front and a smooth bottom surface. The correct size for you will depend on the size of your hand and the scope of the project. What follows is one way you can create the perfect rubber, but if you achieve the same result in a different way that's absolutely fine.

1 Start out with your cotton and wadding in roughly the proportions shown here. I've used a 12in (300mm) rule so you have an idea of scale.

2 Fold the wadding in half and then fold in half again, so that it is now only a quarter of the original size.

3 Take the corner of the loose edges and fold diagonally toward the corner of the folded edges, just shy of making a perfect triangle.

4 Fold the two outer corners into the center, tucking in any loose edges.

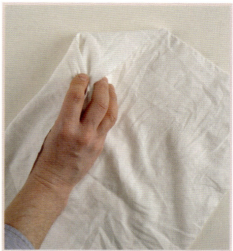

5 Place the wadding on the cotton sheet, pointing into one of the corners, about a third of the way down the square.

6 Pull the corner of the cotton sheet over the point of the wadding and wrap the sides of the cotton into the middle.

8 Wrap the last of the cotton around the heel of the bundle to hold everything together.

7 Repeat with the other side, keeping the bundle nice and tight. Be careful not to allow any creases to form.

9 The remainder of the cotton can be twisted tight and held in the palm of your hand to maintain the shape.

Using a rubber

SUCCESSFULLY applying something as sticky as shellac with a cloth takes some practice. The technique is only possible because the cotton wrap is shaped tightly around the wadding so it is not permitted to slip around on the surface of the polish. French polishing has a lot in common with some other "wet" trades such as painting, lacquering and even plastering in that it requires the user to develop a feel for the medium.

To gauge the level of surface resistance you will experience, there is a simple experiment you can try to mimic the process. With a soft cloth polish a piece of mirror so that it is dust and grease free. Wash your hands and dry them thoroughly then cup them in front of your face to form a mask and huff into them. Using the heel of your hand, attempt to move across the mirror without juddering. This will give you an idea of the amount of pressure required to use the rubber effectively. This test won't work with a completely dry hand.

To load, or charge, the rubber with polish, simply unwrap it and fold back the front corner of the wadding and apply the polish. A brand-new rubber will take quite a lot, and it might need a few tries before you have enough soaked in for

▲ *You can learn the right amount of pressure needed by using a mirror.*

it to work. Press on the sole with your thumb to squeeze the polish to the surface. It just needs to pool around your thumb tip without running down your wrist. There are many theories about the precise nature of the strokes one should make with the rubber, and, as fascinating as it is to learn how others work, their techniques never quite match my own. I'm not suggesting that I am unique in my approach, only that everyone develops a style that suits their own way of working. In short, don't get hung up on whether you should be doing figures of eight, swirls or

▼ *To charge the rubber with polish you will need to unwrap it first.*

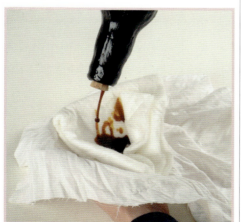

▼ *Use your thumb to test if you have enough polish.*

◀ *A fad is made from skinned wadding and the external skin prevents it leaving fluffy deposits.*

moving in the right direction before it makes contact with the surface. Similarly, make sure you follow through with the stroke at the end and lift off as lightly as you touched down.

Using a fad

A FAD is made from the same material as that used for the inner part of the rubber: skinned wadding. It is the external skin on this sheet of cotton batting that prevents it from breaking down and leaving fluffy deposits all over the surface. A fad should not be used dry, and a fresh piece of wadding requires charging with polish first and squeezing out before it can be used. For this reason it is often best to use the wadding from an existing rubber.

Compared with the rubber, the fad is a slightly coarse method of application and is used in the early stages of polishing either to add color or volume to a finish. Unlike the rubber, a fad does not need to be formed into any particular shape for it to work, but it is advisable to fold the broken edge of the wadding away from the working surface.

straight lines – a combination of everything will get perfect results as long as you aim for an even surface covering and finish with straight strokes. More important is never to stop dead on the surface or start by plonking the rubber down. Glide into the stroke so the rubber is

Using oil to lubricate the rubber

There are plenty of polishers who routinely use oil to lubricate the rubber so that they can work the surface for longer periods of time. Clear mineral oil can be flicked from the fingers onto large surfaces or dabbed onto the sole of the rubber. This is a useful technique to master, but it does require you to remove any trace of the oil before anything like a shine can be achieved. We will look at ways to achieve this later (see Finishing off on page 80).

▶ *Clear mineral oil can be dabbed onto the sole of the rubber to lubricate it.*

Pro Tip

Brushwork

If carried out well, you will find that there should be no need to sand flat between your coats of shellac, and this is quite achievable if each step of the process is completed using either a fad or a rubber. When you are starting out it is likely that you will reach for the brush more often than not, so it is advisable that you develop good brush skills in order to save time removing brush lines later after the polish has dried.

THERE is little call for paintbrushes when it comes to applying shellac (it's best to use a polishing mop) but natural bristle brushes are recommended for the application of oil stains and stipples. As with all wet-finish applications, the best results are achieved if runs and drips are avoided. To do this, get used to charging the brush sparingly and only ever half way up the bristles. On a flat surface, avoid starting a stroke directly on the edge, and lift off as you reach the other side. Shellac dries quickly, unlike oil-based finishes which can be laid on the surface and then straightened out with the tip of the bristles – the long drying time allows the product to flow smooth and level.

With shellac you get one or two passes if you're lucky before it dries and becomes unworkable. So, when you pick up the brush, make sure you mean business, and be confident with the strokes regardless of the size of the area to be finished.

▼ *Don't start a stroke with the bristles against an edge…*

▼ *…because the result will be an unsightly run.*

▲ *Touch the brush down on the surface, as close to the edge as you can...*

▲ *...then apply pressure to spread the bristles as you move the brush away from the edge.*

▼ *On the return stroke complete the pass and run off the edge lifting the brush as you go.*

▼ *Small brushes are sometimes the only way to get polish into shaped or molded work.*

▲ *Polishing mops have fine natural bristles.*

▼ *After cleaning, shape the bristles to a point.*

Polishing mop

A MOP is similar in shape to a fitch used for decorating, but the bristles don't come to a point. It has a round handle with a round-shaped soft bristle. Both are available in different sizes, and when laid on the work splay out in a fan shape. When new, the bristles compact to a fine chisel edge and are perfect for working away from corners and where a fad or rubber would struggle to gain access.

Over time the bristles will wear, and what used to be a sharp brush will only be good for flat-surface work and perhaps applying stipple. A fresh mop should be charged with polish and used over a piece of scrap to remove any loose hairs before using in earnest for the first time. After use, clean in denatured alcohol, reshape the bristles into a point and store with bristles pointing upwards. The brush will then set hard and require soaking in denatured alcohol or

Your fine-brush collection

Have to hand some of the finest artist's brushes available for touching up small repairs where the surrounding grain pattern can be imitated to cover the repair.

polish before it can be used again. Don't be tempted to speed the softening process up by forcing the brush into the bottom of the jar. This will damage the bristles causing loose fibers to stick to the surface when you next use it.

Picking out

THE term *picking out* is used to describe the process of selecting specific areas for coloring or touching up. Depending on the size of the area that needs attention, this can be done with an artist's round brush or a mop. A brush will lay a great deal more polish than a fad or a rubber, so make sure the color solution is fairly weak if the amount of adjustment is slight.

More than one brush coat will result in a higher build-up of polish with raised dark edges that are hard to disguise.

▼ *Mops can be used to gain access where a rubber or fad cannot be used.*

Flatting off between coats

One of the benefits of choosing shellac for a finish is that you can control the color, tone, depth of finish and shine as you go along. For this reason, cutting back between coats requires you to have a light hand and a good eye. If your surface is flat and without any details such as moldings, flatting will be precisely that. But if the surface is shaped in any way, as you will find on an old piece of furniture, flatting is really smoothing.

USING a hard block wrapped with abrasive paper on a less-than-perfect surface will result in rubbing through one layer to the next and creating lighter areas. To avoid this happening, wrap the abrasive around your fingers and work the surface gently, usually in the direction of the grain.

Imperfections are best viewed by getting down to the same level as the surface.

Checking the surface is level

FOR a dead-flat finish you will want to check for a level surface throughout the process of bodying up, or building up the layer of shellac. To do this you will have to get down almost to the same level as the surface and look straight across, focusing along the line of sight with light from all directions, a process sometimes referred to as "raking light."

Over-sanding can cut through the polish.

Checking for flatness with abrasive papers

Aʟᴇɴᴛʟᴇ wipe over with a fine abrasive paper will reveal imperfections that were not obvious while a surface was shiny. The polish has to be dry and produce fine dust if flatting with abrasive paper is to be successful. Particular care needs to be taken on moldings and edges, as it is easy to remove more polish and therefore color to these areas. In most cases you will need to work in the same direction as the grain with papers of 240-grit or above. It is not until you reach 400-grit and above that you can follow a circular motion without the risk of leaving a scratch pattern.

▶ *Be careful not to remove more polish than you intend to at the edges of flat work and moldings.*

Good use of light

Take care when using strip lights to detect imperfections in the surface. Very different effects show up when the light is running in the direction of the grain compared with when it is positioned across the grain.

▼ *A surface viewed with strip lights running in the direction of the grain.*

▼ *The same surface viewed with strip lights positioned across the grain.*

Finishing off

The final few passes of the rubber are what will determine the degree of shine and clarity of the finish you achieve. The use of oil will greatly ease the pull of the rubber and enable you to apply more polish at any one time, but it has to be removed before the job can be considered complete. There are some quaint old recipes for this job, including one that recommends using a dilute solution of sulfuric acid with Vienna chalk.

Out of curiosity I tried it some time ago, and it certainly seems to work, but there are other methods that are far more user-friendly and avoid the need to store any more hazardous chemicals safely than those you already have in the workshop.

Stiffing

STIFFING requires the least amount of skill to master. Using the same rubber charged with a half-and-half blend of polish and denatured alcohol, make perfectly straight strokes over the surface without any oil. The rubber will leave a smear behind as the extra alcohol removes the oil from the surface. A lighter touch than normal is required, as too much pressure will fuse the rubber with the surface, leaving you with some cutting back to do when the polish has dried.

You will find that only two or three passes are required – any more would suggest that you may have been a little too generous with the oil. As you progress, the pull on the rubber increases as the oil is removed until the motion becomes distinctly stiff. The name given to the technique now becomes quite clear.

Spiriting off

SPIRITING off is a two-stage process and a rather more advanced technique, so perhaps not one that you should attempt until you are completely confident with the French-polishing process. It requires the use of a hard rubber, preferably made from an existing one, so that it is not soft. You want something akin to a cork

▲ *The alcohol reacts with the oil to cause cloudiness.*

block but not quite as firm. Rinse the wadding and cotton wrap in denatured alcohol to remove all traces of polish from both and leave to dry.

Remake the rubber and add a further wrap of the finest cotton linen you can find. Spiriting off is intended to give a really high gloss, so pay attention to the flatness of the surface before you begin, as any imperfections will be highlighted. It may be necessary to cut back gently with some 600-grit wet-and-dry paper and mineral spirits.

▲ *It may be necessary to cut back with some 600-grit wet-and-dry paper and mineral spirits.*

▲ *The result really is a mirror finish.*

Start off by charging the rubber with a half-and-half mix of polish and denatured alcohol, then flick a small amount of oil on the surface of the polish and begin with small circular strokes followed by straight ones at regular intervals. Rather than burnishing the surface, the process

has the effect of flattening the shellac while it is still relatively soft and pliable. The extra denatured alcohol in the polish ensures it stays soft while the oil acts as a lubricant.

You will need to maintain firm and constant pressure throughout this stage across the entire surface if you are to achieve a uniform shine when the oil has been removed. The next stage needs to be carried out immediately and begins by dropping a small puddle of denatured alcohol on the back of a clean piece of abrasive paper and dipping the rubber into it.

With light pressure this time, make large strokes, in sweeping figures of eight rather than tight circles. The oil trace left behind the rubber becomes cloudy at first, then, as the oil evaporates like steamy breath on a cold day, the surface will become mirror-like. The process can be taken a stage further by dipping the rubber into Vienna chalk and continuing with smooth straight strokes.

◀ *Vienna chalk is used as the final stage in the process.*

Burnishing

A QUICK fix for all dull surfaces is to use burnishing creams and what are commonly sold as revivers. These are more popular with restorers than conservators, as they can easily contaminate some finishes and harbor more dirt and grime in the long run. However, burnishing can come in handy to completely smooth over a surface midway through the process of polishing.

Burnishing creams or pastes come in various levels of abrasive, and they should be used only when you are absolutely certain that there is an adequate thickness of polish to withstand removal of part of the layer. With this in mind, it is advisable to use only the finest compounds and steer clear of any coarse-grade products.

In a powdered form, rottenstone is an ideal product to use either partway through or at the end of the job. A piece of felt made into a pad is used in conjunction with a small amount of mineral spirits or mineral oil, and the rottenstone dabbed onto the pad to rub over the surface. Rottenstone can also be added to wax polish to achieve a soft, aged shine to new polish on an old piece.

▲ *A piece of felt made into a pad is used with a small amount of mineral spirits or mineral oil and the rottenstone.*

Finishing wax

W HEN it comes to finishing wax, it is far easier to buy ready-made compounds, and in most cases these are quite adequate. Every polisher I have met has his own favorite brand and, no doubt, so will you when you have tried out a few different makes. Better still is to blend your own from materials that are easily sourced from specialist suppliers. To do this, you will need a bain-marie, a container suspended in water that can be heated sufficiently to melt the wax with the relevant solvent. Electronic versions of this are available, sold primarily for the use of hot animal glues. This may sound like more trouble than it's worth, but it will give you complete control over the type of wax at your disposal. A hard wax will buff to a higher

shine but will be difficult to apply. A soft wax is easy to apply but will not shine up as well. The secret to achieving a good wax finish is not to apply too much in the first place. Unlike shellac and other varnishes, wax cannot be built up in layers to form a thick coating. The application of waxes can be improved by using a cloth made damp with mineral spirits to flatten the wax.

▶ *Burnishing creams or pastes are available in various levels of abrasive.*

The following three recipes are ones used by renowned conservator Yannick Chastang and offer a range of options.

Soft wax This blend produces a wax with a pleasant smell. It does not offer much protection but wets bare wood sufficiently and is a general wax, particularly useful for interiors and drawers. It is for solid, unvarnished wood only and is acidic, so it must not be used on metal.
- 7oz (200g) beeswax
- 3½oz (100g) mineral spirits
- 10½oz (300g) turpentine

Hard wax This wax is suitable for new pieces or for imparting a high shine to antiques. It offers a good level of protection and is good to use if you are restoring for dealers. Like the soft-wax recipe, it is acidic and should not be used on metal. This wax can be applied on top of a shellac finish.
- 7oz (200g) beeswax
- 3½oz (100g) shellac wax
- 7oz (200g) mineral spirits
- 3½oz (100g) turpentine

Medium-hard wax This is a blend that will offer good protection but cannot be burnished to a high shine. It is very useful for antiques that are part of a collection, as it will allow the newly conserved piece to blend with the old. This wax should be applied on top of a shellac finish or polish. It is also acidic and should not be used on metal.
- 7oz (200g) beeswax
- 2oz (60g) shellac
- 5⅓oz (150g) mineral spirits
- 5⅓oz (150g) turpentine

Microcrystalline wax This product can be used on its own, but it remains very soft. It can be combined with mineral spirits, and, although it can be used on top of a shellac finish, it will remain matte. Unlike the other recipes, it is safe to use on metal and is generally favored by conservators.

▲ *Blend your own wax in a bain-marie, which is a container suspended in water that can be heated.*

▲ *Electronic versions of bains-marie are sold primarily for the use of hot animal glues.*

Pro Tip

Using a rubber to apply hard wax

Extremely hard compounds can be smoothed flat with a rubber and mineral spirits in exactly the same way as French polish. Make a rubber as you would for shellac and charge it with mineral spirits instead of shellac. Don't overwork the surface, or you will only succeed in removing the wax. When the wax is dry, provided that the surface will withstand it, polish off with a buffing machine.

Cleaning and repolishing

6

Rejuvenating a piece of furniture

In some respects, the best way to get started with French polishing is to work on a piece of furniture that already has a reasonable finish. The process of French polishing is virtually unique, in that polish applied today will adhere to polish that was first applied a century or more ago. Provided that the original surface is still intact, there is no need to strip it off and start from scratch. In fact, this should only ever be considered as a last resort and with the advice of an expert.

THE charm, and a great deal of the monetary value, of a piece of antique furniture is contained within the patina that has taken many years to develop, so this should be protected as a matter of course.

Conservation or restoration

MANY people think that there is no clear distinction between these two approaches to handling antique furniture, but in fact the techniques are worlds apart. Conservators are primarily concerned with protecting what is already there with a minimum amount of intervention. It is of the utmost importance to them that the treatments they carry out are reversible and not likely to degrade the piece further in any way.

In contrast, the restorer will attempt to bring the piece back to a fit state to function in the capacity for which it was originally conceived. The work of the restorer can be invasive and, however well intentioned their efforts, the results raise questions of ethics and best practice. Of course, one could take the view that such work is the ultimate in recycling.

▲ *This mahogany window seat dates from between 1830 and 1837.*

Testing for French polish

1 Dampen a cotton bud with denatured alcohol.

2 Gently apply the denatured alcohol to an inconspicuous area that can be identified as having the finish.

3 Take a second cotton bud and dampen with mineral spirits.

4 Gently apply the mineral spirits alongside the first test area.

5 With a clean cloth wipe once over the two test areas at the same time. If the finish is shellac, only the denatured alcohol will remove the polish.

6 As mineral spirits will leave your original finish in place if it is shellac, you can use it to clean the surface, confident that the original finish will remain intact.

Identifying the finish

For this project I have chosen to work on a William IV mahogany window seat, dating from between 1830 and 1837. The proportions are dainty, as one would expect from a piece of this period – the decorative Regency style had not yet made the transition into the more robust forms of Victorian furniture.

The scrolled ends of the seat are held in place with large steel screws through a substantial underframe, suggesting an awareness of the type of engineering that would shape the latter half of the 19th century. We know that shellac finishing was first introduced to Britain by French cabinet makers during the first quarter of the 19th century as an alternative to wax and oils, so the likelihood is that this piece was originally finished with shellac.

To be certain, though, there is a simple test that can be carried out on an inconspicuous part of the piece (see "Testing for French polish" above). Once you are confident the finish is shellac, you can proceed with cleaning the surface using mineral spirits. Household detergents should not be used, because these can contain chemicals that will damage the polish. Any products that are routinely sold as revivers should also be avoided for the same reason. In most cases they will have a darkening effect and serve to attract and trap dirt. It is worth noting that in the world of conservation distilled water is one of the preferred solutions for removing dirt and grime and therefore an indication of just how delicate some finishes are and how susceptible they can be to unintentional damage.

Structural integrity

THERE is nothing terribly complex about the design of this piece, and careful inspection suggests that it has never been repaired or badly treated. There are some stains on the seat, but this is no surprise given its age. To remove these would involve removing the original finish,

▼ Use steel wool or abrasive pads to remove old wax.

which could never be satisfactorily restored, so the decision was made to leave things as they are and love this piece "warts an' all." Credit should go to the original craftsman, as there was only one loose mortise-and-tenon joint out of eight. It was just possible to inject some hide glue into the joint, clamp it firm and reseat some of the original glue blocks holding the seat in place.

Removing the old wax

USING the finest grade of steel wool or, better still, an abrasive pad, gently rub over the surface, treating small areas at a time to remove the build-up of wax and grime. In some instances, abrasives will be too aggressive, and clean cloths should be used instead, especially if you are preparing the piece for sale. If in doubt, the less removed the better. Continue to work in small areas and remove the dirt with a succession of clean cloths. Follow up with a wipe over with a clean cloth dampened with mineral spirits.

▲ Use clean cloths to remove the dirt.

Applying fresh shellac

FOLLOWING the instructions given in Chapter 5 (see page 72), take your rubber and begin to wipe over the surface as if starting from scratch. I used garnet polish here, as its rich, dark tones replaced some of the color that had been removed during cleaning, and I made no attempt to correct the color. This particular piece of furniture gets used extensively as a makeshift coffee table, so the seat area was treated with a few more layers of polish than the rest. Fortunately, it was not in need of repairs short of a loose glue block underneath, so the makeover was quite quick.

▶ Apply fresh shellac – the rich tones of garnet polish replace some of the color removed during cleaning.

Waxing off

Perhaps in its original state this seat may well have been left with a full shine, but that's not appropriate unless you want your antique to look brand new. To achieve a more satin effect, wax can now be applied with fine-grade steel wool or a soft cloth when the polish has been left to dry overnight. A light touch is required if you don't want to remove the fresh polish. Depending on the temperature of your workshop, leave the wax to dry on the surface; it will appear matte. If the wax is at all lumpy or too thick in some areas, straighten it out with a clean cloth dampened with mineral spirits before buffing off with a soft cloth. The end result is a cleaner version of the original with a protective wax coating and retaining all the authentic signs of ageing.

▼ *Apply wax with fine-grade steel wool or a soft cloth.*

▼ *If the wax is lumpy or too thick, straighten it out with a clean cloth dampened with a little mineral spirits.*

Adding patina with wax and pigments

If, after all your efforts, you feel that you may have overdone things and cleaned away more of the patina than you might have wished, do not despair. Try blending a small amount of dark-earth pigment (black or brown umber) with your wax before applying. The effect is slightly smoky and will help to restore the appearance of decades of use.

◀ *Buff the surface with a soft cloth.*

▲ *The restored window seat.*

Solutions

Whatever difficulties you encounter, our troubleshooting guide has all the answers.

Repairing old polish

Shellac is the only surface treatment that can be repaired reliably by applying the same product that was used originally. It is also the best product to use when repairing other finishes that are not shellac or alcohol-based. To demonstrate how various repairs can be made, we have used two pieces of furniture, a 1930s trolley and a 19th-century table. Both pieces have a number of surface defects that can be repaired in similar ways with either hard wax, polish or even new pieces of wood.

THIS piece, Trolley No. 901, designed by Finnish designer Alvar Aalto, was produced around 1936. Shellac was still a popular finish at the time, but synthetic lacquers were becoming increasingly popular, and this was finished with a synthetic product. Items such as this were cutting-edge designs, produced in quantity using all that the technology of the day had to offer.

▶ *The synthetic lacquer on the trolley shows signs of water damage, and there are areas where the finish has completely disappeared.*

In contrast, our second example piece is a small drop-leaf table from the latter end of the 19th century. Close inspection indicates that it has been restored on more than one occasion, but there is plenty to suggest that the original finish is largely still intact. All things considered, we can be confident that the finish is shellac and alcohol based.

▶ *The table has sustained damage to one or two edges, and there is a very noticeable difference in color between the leaves of the table.*

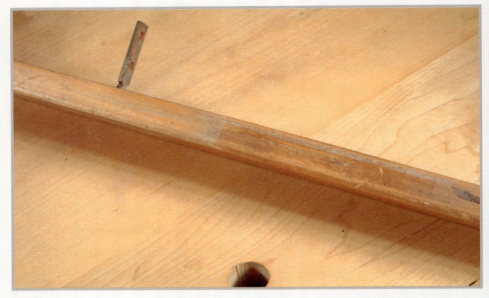

▲ *The area on the left has been cleaned, while the area on the right has not.*

Cleaning an existing surface finish

THE same process can be used to clean both shellac and synthetic lacquers. Using either a proprietary dewaxing solution or mineral spirits, wipe over the surface with a soft cloth and then remove the dirt and grime with a clean one.

You may need to be a little more aggressive with your cleaning and use the finest grade of steel wool to remove some dirt. Do exercise a little caution here if you are working on an old item, as much of its monetary value is contained within the original finish, however it may jar with your standards as a perfectionist.

▶ *Using either a proprietary dewaxing solution or mineral spirits, wipe with a soft cloth.*

Removing the dirt, grease and wax will not only prepare the surface for a fresh coat of polish, it will also allow you to assess the damage and decide what steps to take to put them right.

Hiding stains

Our table had some rather unpleasant stains on the top that needed attention. A combination of spilled liquid and an attempt to rectify the damage had removed part of the existing finish.

Look closely at any piece of wood, however plain, and there will be evidence of a grain pattern. By recognizing the pattern we can use it to help us add color to an area without it looking obvious. Spirit colors are best suited to this technique, as they remain transparent and allow the light

to react with the grain. Start by applying a dilute color to the affected area to bring it close to the tones around it. Then mix a color, preferably darker, that matches the grain tones adjacent to the repair.

Gently extend the pattern into the repair and beyond, tapering out to nothing. The whole area will need to be sealed over with a rubber of clear shellac to blend it in further with the existing polish.

▶ *Spilled liquid and an unsuccessful attempt to rectify the damage had removed part of the existing finish.*

▼ *Apply a dilute color to the affected area.*

▼ *Gently extend the pattern into the repair and beyond.*

▲ *Hard-wax sticks require heating so that the wax becomes molten.*

Disguising scratches with wax

There are two types of wax used to conceal scratches on an existing finish. Hard-wax sticks are brittle and expensive to buy so should be treated carefully when handled.

They require heating so that the wax becomes molten enough to run freely into the affected area. This can be done by heating up small amounts in a spoon with a lighter or by using a soldering iron or pyrography tool.

When cooled the wax becomes extremely hard, so it is good for exposed edges and table tops, but it is also tricky to blend into the surrounding surface without damaging the polish, so be careful. A sharp chisel can be used with caution, or even fine metal files. Finish off with a fine abrasive paper. Soft waxes can be applied in the same way but tend to shrink back and develop air bubbles that need filling again, so a good trick is to work the wax into the scratch when cold with a wooden spatula.

▼ *Hard-wax fillers can be sanded flat with a fine abrasive paper.*

1 Start by choosing a wax as close in color to the surrounding area as you can.

2 Go darker rather than lighter if a perfect match can't be found.

3 With a fine pick, clean out the hole or scratch to remove any loose material and create a pit in which to push the wax using the rounded edge on the spatula.

4 Turn the tool over to a sharp edge and gently scrape the excess away from the surface.

5 A soft edge scraper made from wood will not scratch the surrounding area when used to remove the excess of wax.

Disguising repairs with polish

There will always be damaged areas that cannot be repaired with wax, and the solution is often to graft on a new piece of wood or veneer. This technique will take some advanced skills in cabinet work and an ability to recognize different woods in order to establish a close match before any finishing is applied.

Pay attention to the grain texture as well as the grain direction and the color.

Experiment with stains to get a close match, this time working lighter if an exact match cannot be found.

Garnet polish applied with a brush was just enough to color the new piece to match with the surrounding wood, and, having achieved the right color, the grain was filled with more brush coats of clear shellac then finished with a rubber over the entire panel to blend in the repair further.

Similar repairs can often require some fine tuning, and this can be done by adding either spirit-based colors or earth pigments to shellac and painting onto the repair. Using the back of an old piece of abrasive paper, mix the pigments with shellac by adding just a few grains at a time. Test each time you make an adjustment, because you will want to make only one or two strokes with the brush on the repair.

The easiest match can sometimes be found in the range of polishes you already have on the shelf, such is the versatility of shellac.

The bare sections of molding on the trolley were matched to the existing lacquer with only a single brush stroke of button polish.

▼ *Experiment to get a match. The oil stain used here was labeled Light Oak but the table is mahogany, showing the best match may not be found in the product name.*

▼ *With a brush, apply just enough garnet polish to color the new piece to match the surrounding wood.*

▼ *Fill the grain with more brush coats of clear shellac, then finish with a rubber over the entire panel.*

Add either spirit-based colors or earth pigments to shellac to fine-tune your repair.

I used raw and burnt sienna with French polish to color match this repair.

▼ *The molding on the trolley was matched to the existing lacquer with only a single brush stroke of button polish.*

Removing water marks

Water marks are so tricky that it isn't possible to offer just one solution for repairing them. They come in all shapes and sizes and can affect just the polish alone or the wood beneath as well. If caught quickly, the marks will sometimes disappear on their own. If the marks aren't too severe, you can try using burnishing cream to remove them, but this can result in a very shiny patch where the mark used to be. You will need to treat the whole panel or reduce the shine by applying some wax with fine steel wool.

There are methods recorded in old handbooks that recommend the use of some stringent chemicals. These may well be very effective but are not something I would like to encourage when there are other safer options. In a majority of cases, dewaxing the surface and abrading slightly before applying more shellac will deal with the problem, even on synthetic lacquers.

◀ *A rubber of garnet polish was all that was needed to repair an area of water damage to the frame of the trolley.*

Color matching large areas

It is evident that there are differences in color across the three panels that make up the top of this table. It is most likely that the darker leaf has had less exposure to sunlight over time than the other two.

To match these up, we must first consider the color and decide, in this case, which sort of brown we are working with. There is a strong reddish quality to the darker leaf, and this must be our guide for mixing up a color wash. The tone is warm and golden, and the grain changes from light to dark depending on the angle it is viewed from. This tells you that your color wash must be completely transparent, so that this natural response to a change in angle can occur. For this reason, use a pale polish as your base and not button, garnet or French, as these have their own distinct tones.

I like to work with two different colors made from dilute solutions of spirit powder on two separate

▶ *It is likely that the darker leaf (at the back) has had less exposure to sunlight than the other two.*

▲ *Mix colors from dilute solutions of spirit powder on two separate rubbers. This is Bismarck brown.*

▲ *Applying alternate layers of colored polish to the lighter panels will gradually bring the color to match the darker leaf.*

rubbers: the first is Bismarck brown, which has a deep-red quality; the second is Vandyke brown, which has a golden tone. Alternate layers of each colored polish to the lighter panels will gradually bring the color to match the darker leaf. Be careful not to overlap the rubber strokes, as this will introduce stripes, and check progress regularly from all angles. There is an easy way to neutralize too much red by introducing a third rubber of green polish, although this tends to give a slightly muddy appearance to the finish if overused. When you are happy with the color, and to complete the process, use a clear-polish rubber to match the level of finish and the degree of grain filled.

▼ *When you are happy with the color, use a clear-polish rubber to match the level of finish.*

Resolving common problems

For all its quirks, shellac is a very forgiving material to use. However, even if you have done everything right and followed all good practices religiously, there will be times when things don't go as well as they should. Here are the most common problems and how to deal with them.

The polish is too thick

You'll know if your polish is too thick because it will not leave the brush evenly or bleed through the cotton wrap of your rubber evenly. By squeezing the rubber or tightening the wrap too much the polish leaks out at the heel of the rubber. You are most likely to encounter polish that is too thick to apply easily if you are mixing your own. There's an easy fix for this: just add more denatured alcohol and stir. This works just as well for ready-made polish, but you should perhaps question the age of the polish and whether it has been stored without a tight-fitting lid.

Too much polish in the rubber

For the beginner, there is a real temptation to overcharge the rubber with polish. Try to resist this, because the result will be a raised trace line of polish behind the rubber as you pass over the surface. If you notice this quickly, you might be able to smooth the line straight away, but my advice is to stop, let the polish harden sufficiently and sand flat with abrasive. Excess polish will also spill out through the cotton wrap as you re-form the rubber and will gel on the outside, possibly sticking to the work.

The rubber is sticking to the surface

A RUBBER that sticks to the surface could indicate that it needs recharging or that the build-up of polish is such that it's not dry enough to allow you to apply any more. The rubber will judder across the surface leaving imprints behind. You will encounter this more often when working on small areas such as box lids or small table tops. The best remedy is to stop and allow the surface to dry and then sand flat with a fine abrasive before continuing. Alternatively, the rubber can be lubricated with a small amount of clear mineral oil (see the Pro Tip in Chapter 5, page 73, for more on how to do this).

The rubber leaves blobs of thick polish behind

THIS is most certainly caused by overcharging the rubber or squeezing it so tightly that it expresses more polish than needed to complete the pass. It is fine to reposition the wadding within the cotton wrap and reshape the rubber as long as the work is presented with a clean area of cloth. While you are doing this it is likely that the deposits will have begun to gel, so any attempt to wipe them away will further damage the surface. The best course of action is to let them harden fully and smooth them out with fine abrasive.

The rubber leaves a scratch pattern behind

S CRATCHES or tramlines left in the polish after the pass are likely to be caused by a speck of dirt either on the rubber or the surface itself. You may also have caught the rubber on a sharp corner and torn the cotton so making the sole uneven. The worst time for this to happen is when you are applying a color, because thin traces of the colored polish will have been removed. So it is important to keep the rubber surface free from scratchy particles and in good all-round condition.

▲ *White water-based stains are a good way of maintaining a china-white appearance on maple and sycamore.*

Uneven tones when using troublesome woods

MAPLE

For the most part, the techniques we have discussed thus far for staining and coloring are suitable for use on most woods, but there are a couple of species to watch out for that have a reputation for turning out blotchy as soon as any finish is applied. Maple is one such wood, and, although this is chosen primarily because of its light color, you may have a good reason to alter its tone. Any stain (oil-, water- or spirit-based) applied straight to the surface will, more often than not, cover in uneven tones.

This is largely because of the tight nature of the grain and the after-effects of machining. This impenetrable surface can be opened up by wetting before sanding, but still the results can be unpredictable. It is therefore recommended that a pre-stain sealer be applied. There are ready-made solutions available, but it is just as easy to make your own from a half-and-half mix of either shellac sanding sealer or white polish and denatured alcohol. This solution can be brushed on and sanded smooth afterwards. At this point, of course – and remembering the rules for product compatibility – the only stain suitable will be an oil-based one. Penetration will be impaired, so be prepared to wipe any excess off the surface before it can form a thin film. My preferred method for keeping a china-white tone on maple and sycamore is to apply a white water stain and finish with a white polish. This will minimize greatly any yellowing of the wood.

CHERRY

The second of our troublesome woods is cherry (pictured right). Highly prized for its lively grain and reflective quality, it can easily become a checkerboard of light and dark blotches (pictured below). The grain structure is less compact than maple, but the most interesting boards feature grain of alternating direction. The light and dark tones are caused by end-grain waves breaking the surface of the board.

Controlled penetration is the key to success with staining cherry, and in the first instance it should be sanded to a much finer grit than, say, mahogany, walnut or oak. A 320-grit or higher paper is recommended, and the extra sanding will, in effect, burnish the surface.

A simple test can be carried out to see if you have a particularly lively sample by wiping over neat denatured alcohol. If the dark patches take noticeably longer to dry than the lighter areas, then you are in for treat when the job is finished. The treatment is the same as for maple. Incidentally, this technique works well if your chosen finish is to be a purely oil-based one.

▲ *A wipe over of denatured alcohol will reveal if you have a piece of cherry with a lively grain structure.*

▼ *Some areas may take noticeably longer to dry.*

Glossary

Abranet the brand name of an open-weave abrasive sheet material produced by Mirka

Alcohol the solvent for all shellac polishes. Available as a clear solution (denatured alcohol) or with a purple dye added (methylated spirits)

Bain-marie a two-part container with one part containing hot water and the other suspended in it

Bodying up the process of adding polish with a rubber or fad to build up an appropriate layer of finish

Burnishing a technique that involves rubbing with a cloth, often with an abrasive compound to increase or reduce shine

Button polish a rich, dark shellac polish produced in circular, disk-like buttons

Carnauba wax a hard wax produced from the leaves of the carnauba tree

Charged the term given to a rubber or fad that is sufficiently impregnated with polish

Cut back lightly abrading a surface to remove minor imperfections prior to another layer of finish

Danish oil a hard-drying finishing oil made up from a blend of tung and linseed oil, and solvent

Denatured alcohol clear ethanol with added chemicals that make it unfit for human consumption

De-nibbing flattening off the surface of a layer of finish with a fine abrasive prior to adding another coat

Dewaxing cleaning the surface of a finish to remove all traces of wax and oil

Fad a sheet of skinned wadding neatly folded to fit the polisher's palm to apply shellac

Fuming the process used to darken woods with high levels of tannin by exposure to the fumes emitted by ammonia

Garnet polish a rich, dark brown shellac polish used mainly on dark woods

Gilding size a treacle-like adhesive used by gilders to lay gold leaf

Glaze an opaque mixture of dark-colored polish used to imitate the signs of age on new work

Glue squeeze-out excess glue that forms outside a joint when the mating parts are brought together

Hard-wax oil a slow-drying blend of hard-drying wax and oils including linseed oil, sunflower oil, jojoba oil, beeswax, carnauba wax and candelilla wax for creating a hard, durable and water-repellent finish

Heart wood the older growth of wood generally used for all construction purposes due to its greater stability over sap wood

Hide glue adhesive made from animal parts

Hypoallergenic a term used to describe a product that is likely to cause fewer allergic reactions

Knotting a shellac-based product used as a barrier on the knots of resinous soft woods to prevent discoloration caused by resin leaching out after the top coat (usually paint) has been applied

Lac the resinous secretion of a number of species of insect that is the basis of shellac polish

Laccifer lacca an aphid-like insect

Linseed oil a clear yellowish oil obtained from the dried ripe seeds of the flax plant, also known as flaxseed oil

Matte a surface that has little or no gloss or shine

Medullary rays the silver-like flecks often found on the face of quarter-sawn wood (mainly oak)

Methylated spirits denatured alcohol (ethanol) with a purple dye added to render it unfit for human consumption

Mineral spirits (white spirit) a clear petroleum-based product sometimes sold as substitute for turpentine

Nitrocellulose lacquers a quick-drying solvent-based lacquer best applied with a spray gun

Patina a slightly tarnished sheen to the surface of a finish that is only achieved over time

Picking out the term used to describe the process of selecting specific areas for coloring or touching up

Pigment any dry mineral that can be added to a coating, stain or filler. Generally held in suspension and not dissolved

Polymerization any process in which relatively small molecules, called monomers, combine chemically to produce a very large chainlike or network molecule (molecular bonding)

Quarter-sawn the term used to describe wood that is cut exactly radially (toward the heart of the log), i.e., at right angles to the growth rings

Raking light a light source that is projected almost parallel to the surface of that being inspected

Rubber (or pad) tightly bound fist-sized piece of wadding wrapped with a fine cotton outer layer

Sandarac a resin obtained from the cypress-like sandarac tree used as a finish for wooden objects before shellac

Sanding sealer a cloudy polish containing fine talc to aid the process of sanding after application, used to seal wood between coats of stain or to raise the grain further to achieve a smooth surface

Sap wood new growth found on wood, usually lighter in color. Generally considered inferior to heart wood

Seed-lac seed-like pellets of shellac produced in the early stages of refining that contain many impurities

Shellac the resin secreted by the female lac bug on trees in the forests of India and Thailand

Skinned wadding soft cotton batting with an outer skin to prevent it from breaking up when used

Solvent the liquid in which solids or resins are dissolved to enable them to be applied in a thin layer

Spiriting off a two-stage process that requires the use of a hard rubber to work the surface of a shellac finish

Stearate zinc-based chemical added to fine abrasive paper to reduce clogging. Also added to sanding sealer

Steel wool a bundle of strands of soft steel threads available in various degrees of abrasiveness

Stick-lac the twigs or small branches on which the shellac resin is attached

Stiffing the process of removing oil from the surface of a shellac finish

Stipple a semi-opaque color wash used to add color to a surface and not stain

Tack rags soft cloth rags impregnated with a sticky oil used to wipe the surface of a sanded area and retain the dust particles

Tannin a biomolecule found in greater quantities in oak than in other timbers

Teak oil the generic name given to a blend of oils and solvent to protect teak. In most cases the solvents used have the opposite effect as they break down the natural oils present in the wood already

Tung oil oil from the nuts of the tung tree

Turpentine an oil created from the sap of pine trees that has a very distinctive smell

UV resistant being resistant to ultraviolet light or sunlight which will cause non-resistant surfaces and materials to discolor

Suppliers

About the author

Many thanks to the following UK companies for supplying the products used in this book.

John Myland Ltd
26 Rothschild Street
London SE27 0HQ
Tel: +44 (0)208 6709161
www.coloursoflondon.co.uk
www.mylands.co.uk

Liberon Limited
Learoyd Road
Mountfied Industrial Estate
New Romney
Kent TN28 8XU
Tel: +44 (0)1797 367555
www.liberon.co.uk

The following companies supply French polishing materials in the USA.

Shellac Finishes
www.shellacfinishes.com

Homestead Finishing Products
www.homesteadfinishingproducts.com

Lee Valley Tools
www.leevalley.com

Fiddes-USA
www.fiddes-usa.com

Derek Jones began his career in furniture making as an apprentice in a restoration workshop in Brighton, UK. What, at 15 years old, felt like an insufferable amount of time spent cleaning old furniture and removing layers of thick sticky varnish, was in fact time well spent. Observing the complete range of finishes with all their faults was a fantastic opportunity to develop an understanding of color, grain texture and construction first hand.

More than a decade later this experience brought him into contact with Paul Richardson, later to become the founding editor of *Furniture & Cabinetmaking* magazine, who described him as "the best polisher I've ever met."

Design and making of bespoke furniture and joinery were Derek's primary focus for the next decade, combining both disciplines with an eye for a good finish. The opportunity came in 2009 to become the editor of *Furniture & Cabinetmaking* magazine himself, and with it a request to write on the subject of French polishing. It seemed only right to take up the challenge that has brought him full circle back to where he started. "It's great to be working with the accumulated knowledge of years of experience but nothing compares to the excitement and enthusiasm experienced when you're desperate to learn a new skill," says Derek.

Derek would like to thank Michael Huntley for being "an extra pair of eyes" on this book.

Index

A

abrasives
  open-weave sheets 40–41
  papers 24, 39, 41, 47, 79
  steel wool 23, 40, 88, 109
absorption rates 45, 51
ageing technique 62–63
air cleaners 20–21
alcohol 28, 35, 108
aluminium oxide paper 39
amber varnish 26, 29
ammonia solution 37, 58
aniline dyes 14, 35 *see also* spirit-
  based stains
animal glues 32, 48, 82, 83, 108
ash 44, 64, 65

B

bains-marie 82, 83, 108
beeswax 13
belt sanders 48
bodying up 26, 29, 78, 108
brushes 22, 23, 74, 77
brushwork 74–77
buffing 13, 22, 82, 83, 90, 91
burnishing 47, 82, 83, 107, 108
burrs 47, 48
button polish 27, 61, 63, 102, 108

C

cabinet scrapers 50–51
card scrapers 51
carnauba wax 13, 108
cellulose finishes 14, 41, 58
charging 104, 108
Chastang, Yannick 83
chemical staining 37
cherry 107
chestnut 44
cleaning, surfaces 87–88, 96
close-grain hardwoods 44
coarse-grain textures 65
color
  ageing with 62–63
  ebonizing 63–64
  and fillers 30, 32, 33
  matching 20, 30, 33, 56, 64,
    102–103
  and polish 26, 61–62
  and stains 56, 57
  wheels 60
conservation of furniture 86
containers, storage 23–24

continuity of grain 44–45
corrosive liquids 23
cotton waste 22
cross banding 47
cutting back 22, 80, 81, 108

D

Danish oil 12, 108
dark polishes 27
delaminating 17
denatured alcohol
  about 28, 108
  for cleaning 107
  for identifying finishes 87
  for identifying tone 45, 107
  for spiriting off 81
  for stiffing 80
  storage of 23
  as thinning agent 16
de-nibbing 39, 108
dewaxing 96, 102, 108
dents 52
dust 20–21, 53
dyes 14

E

earth pigments 32, 37, 38, 91,101
ebonizing 33, 63–64
equipment 22–24

F

fads 22, 35, 73, 74, 77, 108
fillers 25, 30–32
fine-grain woods 65
finish-sanding 47, 50
finishing off 80–83
finishing wax 82–83
flammable liquids 23
flat scrapers 51
flatting off 78–79
French polish 27, 63, 87
fuming 37, 108

G

garnet polish 27, 61, 63, 89, 100,
  108
gilding size sealer 25, 38, 57, 62,
  108
glazes 62–63, 108
glues 32, 48, 108
grain
  filling 25, 30, 65–67
  patterns 45, 49, 53, 56, 97
  textures 65, 106, 107

H

hand-sanding 50
hard wax
  applying 82, 83, 94
  oil 12, 108
  recipe for 83
  sticks 98
heart wood 45, 108
hide glues 32, 48, 108 *see also*
  animal glues
humidity 20

I

identifying finishes 87
inlays 57–58
insoluble pigments 56

K

knotting 108

L

lac 14, 108
lac beetle (*Laccifer lacca*) 14, 108
lacquers 14, 39, 65, 94
layers, delaminating of 17
light polish 26
lighting 20
linear sanders 49
linseed oil 12, 65, 67, 108
lint-free materials 22, 70

M

mahogany 30, 33, 44, 58, 65
maple 44, 64, 106
masking products 57–58
mechanical sanding 48–49
medium-hard wax 83
medullary rays 44, 108
methylated spirits 28, 108
  see also denatured alcohol
microcrystalline wax 83
mineral oils 73
mineral spirits
  about 28, 109
  for ageing 62
  for cleaning 47, 48, 87, 96
  for identifying finishes 87
  and non-alcoholic sealers 57
  for stipples 37
  as thinning agent 13, 25
moldings 47, 50

N

nitrocellulose lacquers 14, 108

O

oak 30, 37, 44, 58, 65
oil
  finishes 12
  for lubrication 73
  removal of 80–81
oil-based stains 34–35, 56, 57, 58
  applying 74, 106
open-grain woods 44, 65
open-weave sheets 40–41
orange polish 27 *see also* French
  polish
orbital sanders 48

P

paint brushes 22, 23, 74, 77
panels 45, 46, 47, 57, 102–103
patinas 86, 91, 109
petroleum-based products 28, 34
picking out 77, 109
pigments 56, 109
plaster of Paris 30, 65–67
plastic containers 23
polish
  coloring 60–64
  containers for 23–24
  correcting thickness 104–105
  disguising repairs 100
  making 29
  mixing 27
  revivers 30
  types 26–27
polishing mops 22, 74, 76–77
polymerization 17, 109
pre-stain sealers 106
proprietary fillers 30
PVA glue 48

Q

quarter-sawn lumber 44, 109
quartering 47

R

rags 22
raising the grain 53, 56
raking light 78, 109
random-orbital sanders 49
reactive finishes 17
repairs, disguising 100
rottenstone 82
rubbers
  about 22, 109
  causing scratching 105

excess polish in 104
leaving blobs 105
lubricating 105
making 70–71
sticking of 105
technique 72–73, 83

S

sandarac varnish 12, 109
sanders 48–49
sanding 47–50
sanding sealer 25, 38, 57
sap wood 45, 109
satinwood 58
sawdust, as a filler 32
scraping 50–51, 99
scratches 30, 98, 105
sealers 25, 56, 57, 106
seed-lac 15, 109
shellac
  about 12, 13–17, 109
  applying 16, 17, 89
  coloring 60–61
  identifying 87
  making 29
  and masking off 58
  qualities 16, 17, 44
  repairing 94
  shelf-life of 29
silicon carbide paper 39
single-part fillers 31
soda crystals 62
soft wax 83, 98
solid panels 46
solvents 13, 17, 28, 29, 57–58, 109
special pale polish 26
spirit-based stains 35, 57, 58, 61,
  97, 100
spiriting off 80–81, 109
sponge applicators 22
spraying 16
staining, hiding of 97
stains
  about 33
  applying 56–59
  types 34–38
  and uneven tones 100, 106, 107
steaming 52
stearated abrasive paper 41, 109
steel wool 23, 40, 88, 109
stick-lac 14, 15, 109
stiffing 80, 109

stipples 37, 38, 62–63, 74, 109
storage containers 23–24
sunlight 20
surface damage 30, 52
surface preparation 47–53
synthetic lacquers 94

T

tack rags 22, 109
tannin 37, 109
teak oil 12, 109
temperature, working 20
thinning agents 13, 16
tight-grain woods 65
transparent white polish 26
tung oil 12
turpentine 13, 28, 109

U

uneven tones 106
UV resistance 109

V

veneers 47–48
ventilation 20–21

W

wadding 22, 52, 70–71, 73, 109
  cleaning 80
walnut 44, 65, 107
water-based stains 36, 56, 57, 58
water marks 102
wax
  for adding patina 91
  disguising scratches 98
  fillers 30, 31
  finishing 82–83
  polish 13
  removal of 88
waxing off 90
wetting, surface 53
white polish 26
white spirit 28, 109 *see also*
  mineral spirits
wood glue, as a filler 32
wood grain, filling 30
wood selection 44–46, 65,
  106–107
wood types 44, 45
workspaces 20–21

To place an order or to request a catalog, contact:
The Taunton Press, Inc.
63 South Main Street, P.O. Box 5506, Newtown, CT 06470-5506
Tel: (800) 888-8286

www.taunton.com